Night Talks

ALSO BY TERRI KIRBY ERICKSON

Thread Count
Telling Tales of Dusk
In the Palms of Angels
A Lake of Light and Clouds
Becoming the Blue Heron
A Sun Inside My Chest

Night Talks

New & Selected Poems

Terri Kirby Erickson

Press 53
Winston-Salem

Press 53, LLC
PO Box 30314
Winston-Salem, NC 27130

First Edition

Copyright © 2023 by Terri Kirby Erickson

All rights reserved, including the right of reproduction in whole or in part in any form except in the case of brief quotations embodied in critical articles or reviews. For permission, contact publisher at editor@press53.com or at the address above.

Cover Art, "Garden Mist," Copyright © 2022
by Stephen White, from the collection of
Gail and Russell Michael

Cover Design by Claire V. Foxx and Kevin Morgan Watson

Cover art photograph by Jordan Parah at
City Art Gallery, Greenville, NC

Author Photograph by
Kim Shouse Photography

Library of Congress Control Number
2023941580

ISBN 978-1-950413-67-6

*In loving memory of my parents,
Thomas (Tom) and Loretta Kirby,
and my brother,
Thomas (Tommy) Kirby, Jr.*

Acknowledgments

Many thanks to the editors of the following publications where these poems or versions of them have appeared:

"American Life in Poetry": "New Bathing Suit," "Hospital Parking Lot," "Fund Drive," "Sponge Bath"

Atlanta Review: "Lightning Bugs," Publication Prize Winner, International Poetry Competition

Between the Lines Cape Fear River Foundation Chapbook: "Boogie-Woogie," "Road Crew"

Boston Literary Magazine: "Hospital Parking Lot"

Broad River Review: "Pixie Cut," Finalist, 2015 Rash Award in Poetry; "Soleá," Finalist, 2018 Rash Award in Poetry; "The Letter," Honorable Mention, 2021 Rash Award in Poetry

Cacti Fur: "Estaleen"

Carolina Woman Magazine: "Kenmore," Grand Prize Winner, Carolina Woman Writing Contest

Cowboy Poetry: "Oak Tree"

Cutthroat: A Journal of the Arts: "After the Explosion," Winner, 2014 Joy Harjo Poetry Prize

Dead Mule School of Southern Literature: "Oak Tree"

Delta Poetry Review: "Alvin and Ila," "In the Midst of Grief, a Heron," "A Nimble Deer"

Deep South Magazine: "The Old Barn," "Night Fishing on Long Beach Pier," "Goldfinch," "New Day"

Dime Show Review: "The Ophthalmology Specialists' Secondary Waiting Room"

Explore: "Bear Watching in Katmai National Park"

Fourth & Sycamore: "Free Breakfast"

Gwarlingo: "Free Breakfast"

Healing the Divide: Poems of Kindness & Connection: "Fund Drive"

How to Love the World: Poems of Gratitude and Hope: "Angel"

Imagining Heaven Anthology: "Heaven"

Journal of the American Medical Association: 1. "Cling Peaches," Erickson TK. JAMA.2009;302(7):722. doi:10.1001/jama.2009.1056; Copyright © 2009 by the American Medical Association. All rights reserved. 2. "Poem by a Woman with Glaucoma," Erickson TK; JAMA.2021; 326(18):1875. doi:10.1001/jama.2021.12950; Copyright © 2021 by the American Medical Association. All rights reserved.

KAKALAK 2015: "Suppertime"

KAKALAK 2020: "Papa's Chair"

KAKALAK 2021: "The Sam White Special"

KAKAKAK 2022: "Cana"

Light: "Sugar"

NASA (National Aeronautics and Space Administration), *History Program Office News & Notes* (Volume 33, Number 2): "Moon Walk"

Nibble: "Sponge Bath"

North Carolina Literary Review: "Making the Biscuits"

O.Henry Magazine: "Sheller," "A Nimble Deer," "Pigeons"

Old Mountain Press: "Yellow Table"

ONE ART Poetry Journal: "Night Talks" (one of top 10 most read poems for ONE ART in 2020), "The White Bench," "Girl with a Red Ribbon," "The Neighbor's Barn"

One Sentence Poems: "Sorrow Bird"

Paris Voice: "Luncheon in Paris"

Pinesong: "Madison's Picture," Honorable Mention, North Carolina Poetry Society Caldwell Nixon Jr. Contest; "Frank and Alice: A Love Story," First Place, NCPS Poetry of Love Award; "Bloom," Second Place, NCPS Poetry of Courage Award; "At the Drive-In," Third Place, NCPS Mary Ruffin Poole American Heritage Award

Pinestraw: "Pigeons"

Pisgah Review: "County Fair"

Plainsongs: "Fog," Editor's Award Poem

Poetry Foundation: "Hospital Parking Lot," "Sponge Bath," "Fund Drive," "New Bathing Suit"

Poetry in Plain Sight: "Blue Bird," "Empathy," "Red Tractor," "Another Memory of My Mother's Kindness," "My Mother's Cookie Cutters," "Sponge Bath"

Poetry of Presence: An Anthology of Mindfulness Poems, Volume 2: "Sponge Bath," "New Bathing Suit"

Poet's Market: "At the Bowling Alley," Honorable Mention, 2011 Randall Jarrell Poetry Competition

Poets Reading the News: "Geminids"

Quarterly Literary Review Singapore (QLRS): "Hate Crime," "Peony"

Raptor Resource Project: "Bald Eagle"

Red Eft Review: "Breakfast with My Parents"

Salt Magazine: "Sheller," "A Nimble Deer," "Pigeons"

San Pedro River Review: "The Physics of Fishing"

Scythe: "To My Brother Who Died a Virgin"

Shoal: "Shrimp Boat Captain," First Place Poetry, Carteret Writers 19th Annual Writing Contest

Shot Glass Journal: "My Mother's Cookie Cutters," "My Father's Cowboy Boots"

Sport Literate: "The Referee"

Stone Gathering Anthology: "Night Talks"

storySouth: "Loretta Wray," "Red Tractor"

The Avalon Literary Review: "Ironing Clothes Three Months After My Father's Death"

The Christian Century: "Geese," Copyright © 2018 by *The Christian Century*. Reprinted by permission from the August 30, 2018 issue of *The Christian Century*

The Christian Science Monitor: "Queen Anne's Lace"

The Gatherings Project: "The Doctor Who Dies of the Coronavirus After the Hospital Runs Out of Gloves"

The Glaucoma Foundation Newsletter and Marketing Materials: "The Ophthalmology Specialists' Secondary Waiting Room"

The New Verse News: "The Doctor Who Dies of the Coronavirus After the Hospital Runs Out of Gloves" (Nominated for a Pushcart Prize), "Ida," "Winter Morning"

The North Carolina Bluebird Society's *Bluebird Notes*: "Bluebird"

The Ofi Press: "Angel"

The Orchards Poetry Journal: "Laundry Day"

The Path to Kindness: Poems of Connection and Joy: "Free Breakfast," "Night Talks"

The Sixty-Four: Best Poets of 2019: "After the Explosion"

The Southern Poetry Anthology, Volume VII: North Carolina: "Queen Anne's Lace," "Making the Biscuits"

The SUN: "Loving You Burns Like Shingles"

The Wonder of Small Things: Poems of Peace & Renewal: "Goldfinch"

The Writer's Almanac: "Ice Cream Truck"

Third Wednesday: "Egg Salad"

Time of Singing: "Bluebird," Editor's Choice, Summer Poetry Contest

Turtle Island Quarterly: "New Bathing Suit"

27 rue de fleures: "Stevie Santos"

Valparaiso Poetry Review: "Albino Opossum"

Verse Daily: "County Fair," "Red Tractor," "Moon Walk"

Walter: "Pigeons"

Wild Goose Poetry Review: "A Rancher Buries His Wife"

Your Daily Poem: "Autumnal Equinox," "Thread Count," "Shrimp Boat Captain," "Queen Anne's Lace"

Contents

SIRIUS

Night Talks	3

RIGIL KENTAURUS

Night Fishing on Long Beach Pier	7
Queen Anne's Lace	9
Loretta Wray	10
The Letter	11
At the Bowling Alley	12
Brown Dress	13
Free Breakfast	14
Goldfinch	15
Hospital Parking Lot	16
The Old Barn	17
Poem by a Woman with Glaucoma	18
Sheller	19
Stevie Santos	20
Late Summer Blues	21
Sorrow Bird	22
To My Brother Who Died a Virgin	23

ALTAIR

Laundry Day	27
Bluebird	28
The Ophthalmology Specialists' Secondary Waiting Room	29
Making the Biscuits	30
Girl with a Red Ribbon	31
The Referee	32
Frank and Alice: A Love Story	33
Pixie Cut	34

Albino Opossum	35
Moon Walk	36
A Rancher Buries His Wife	37
Stan's Place	38
Sponge Bath	39
Slave Cemetery	40
A Nimble Deer	41
New Bathing Suit	42

ANTARES

The White Bench	45
Ice Cream Truck	46
Kenmore	47
County Fair	48
Gardening Lesson	49
Brilliant Delusion	50
Loving You Burns Like Shingles	51
Soleá	52
Nighthawks	53
Fog	54
Hate Crime	55
Rain	56
At the Poultry Show	58
The Physics of Fishing	59
The Peony	60
After the Explosion	61

VEGA

Breakfast with My Parents	65
Bare Tree in the Afternoon	66
The Doctor Who Dies of the Coronavirus After the Hospital Runs Out of Gloves	67
Empathy	68
Angel	69
Sunrise Avenue	70
Estaleen	71

Heaven	72
Sugar	73
Papa's Chair	74
Thread Count	75
Betty's Roadside Diner	76
Bloom	78
Lightning Bugs	79
Portrait of Elizabeth	80
At the Drive-In	81

ARCTURUS

Washing Dishes	85
Red Tractor	86
At the Cosmetic Counter	87
Autumnal Equinox	88
Sabine LeBlanc	89
Tomato Sandwich	90
Sundays	91
My Father's Cowboy Boots	92
Alvin and Ila	93
Wisteria	94
Egg Salad	95
Shrimp Boat Captain	96
Cling Peaches	97
In the Midst of Grief, a Heron	98
Kingston Mines	99
Geese	100

PROCYON

Suppertime	103
Winter Morning	105
Bear Watching in Katmai National Park	106
Stairway to Heaven	107
The Village Soda Shop	108
Photograph of a Friend	109
Fund Drive	110

My Mother's Cookie Cutters	111
Merry-Go-Round	112
Massage Therapy	113
Luncheon in Paris	114
Ironing Clothes Three Months After My Father's Death	115
Oak Tree	116
Bald Eagle	117
Yellow Table	118
New Day	119

POLLUX

Cana	123
Mallard Lake	124
Ida	125
Poem for My Brother Who Died at Twenty	126
The Neighbors' Barn	127
Boogie-Woogie	128
The Sam White Special	129
Madison's Picture	130
Fawn	131
When I'm with You	132
Road Crew	133
For My Daughter, Turning Forty	134
Pigeons	135
Another Memory of My Mother's Kindness	136
Ode to My New Toaster	137
Play Ball	138
Geminids	140

Bibliography of New & Selected Poems	143
Personal Acknowledgments	147
Author and Cover Artist Biographies	149

*I will love the light for it shows me the way;
yet I will love the darkness for it shows me the stars.*

—Og Mandino

SIRIUS

Night Talks

When one would wake in the night, the other
followed. Then, in their bed, next to their window
that was always open, my mother and father
would talk to the sound of cars going by,
the hum of streetlights, the occasional bark
of a neighbor's dog. They spoke of high school
dances, family vacations, raising children,
being grandparents. And their faces, soft
with age and sleep, were hidden in the dark,
so they could speak at last of their lost son,
without any need to shield each other from
that pain. It must have been a relief to unpack
the shared sadness they courageously carried,
to put it down, if only for an hour. It was like
I could hear them from my own bed
across town, as I slipped into a deeper sleep,
reassured and comforted by their beloved
familiar voices echoing among the stars.

RIGIL KENTAURUS

Night Fishing on Long Beach Pier

Without the loud whoops of children,
their feet pounding the floorboards as
they ran, or the incessant cries of hungry
gulls, what we heard was water sloshing
around the pilings, the hushed voice of
our mother saying, *soon, soon, we'll go
home soon,* as we leaned against her soft
shoulders beneath the green glow of old
fluorescent lights and stars that looked
like tiny tears in the night's dark fabric.
Our father was just a silhouette slouched
against the knife-marked, shrimp-husk-
littered railing, his fishing rod bowed
and gently bobbing as invisible waves
rolled into the shore. A few miles down
the beach, the incoming tide was busy
washing away the sandcastle my brother
and I built in front of the rented cottage
where our grandmother, worn out from
surf fishing since dawn, was sleeping. It
was hours past our bedtime, so our eye-
lids—my brother's and mine—fluttered
like the wings of Luna moths against our
smooth, sunburned cheeks as the night
air ran its salty fingers through our hair.
Still, our father fished on and on. To reel
in his hooks meant some legendary fish
might clamp its jaws around someone
else's bait. But perhaps it was the sight
of his young family huddled on that slim
wooden bench—his wife's face glowing
like a moon-lit slipper shell, his children's
nodding heads as we struggled to stay

awake—that kept him from packing up his gear. Maybe he didn't want it to end, this feeling he couldn't name, so fleeting it was almost gone, already, and nothing anyone can do or say will bring it back.

Queen Anne's Lace

Queen Anne's lace dandies up
a ditch, like embroidered hankies
in a farmer's pocket.

Such tiny seed-pearl petals
seem hand-sewn by
seraphim to their purple

centers—yet they thrive
in common places, fine as tatted
borders, blanket-stitched to burlap.

Loretta Wray

My mother, lipstick red, barefoot, toenails painted
the palest shade of pink, stretched out her dancer's legs
and rubbed suntan lotion into a face
that should have been magnified on a movie screen—
the kind that bowled men over even with curlers in her hair
and children dangling from both hands wherever she went.
They never saw the greasy chaise lounge behind our house
where the sun whispered sonnets in her ears
and darkened her skin with hot kisses while the radio
played "Blue Velvet." And the greengrocer and the mailman
and the gas station attendants and the jean-clad
teenage boys loitering downtown on Saturday afternoons,
who caught glimpses of Loretta Wray every now
and then, if they were lucky, would have dropped dead with desire
if they'd seen her sunning herself in our backyard wearing
nothing but a two-piece bathing suit and a lazy, sun-drenched
grin, the best years of her life almost, but not quite, past.

The Letter

Nothing is ordinary—not condensation on a pane
of glass—that streak of sunlight, yellow
as lemons, in the neighbor's backyard. Trees

are rustling tender new leaves, and our lawn
is as thick as a wool rug. Even the scent of coffee

wafting from the kitchen is a miracle,
a woman walking her little dog down the sidewalk,
its leash as taut as rigging. Yet, every house

hides something that hurts, even as we call to one
another, *good morning, good morning*—

our faces open as a letter lying on a table, the kind
that makes our hands shake when we find it
in the mailbox, that we read only once.

At the Bowling Alley

Blind, the old man still beats you. He holds
the heavy ball as if it's made of Styrofoam, pitches
it down the alley and stands there, listening for
the strike. You marvel that this dreg of humanity
with his hawk-nosed face and unwashed body,
tattoos dripping down the slack skin of his arms
and between the lizard-like folds of his scrawny
neck, wins every game. The fact that he's blind,
too, is the final insult since you can spot a fly
circling a cup of greasy French fries from across
the dang building—the barrettes in Missy Cardwell's
curly blonde hair as she's walking to the restroom
at the far-end of the hall, her short skirt swinging
from side to side in that flirty way of hers that drives
you half-crazy. Maybe that's it—the old man has no
distractions. There's nothing but the feel of the ball
in his hands, the squeak of his beat-up bowling shoes
on the polished floor, and the sound of ten pins knocked
down in one fell swoop, hit so hard you wonder if
they'll ever get up. And even worse, he's your father,
the same sorry guy who took off when you were six.
You know he knows who you are, but he never
says a word—just whips the living fool out of you
and walks away, as if you're just another loser.

Brown Dress

When I was a little girl,
I wanted to wear the same dress
every day. It was brown plaid
with a scalloped collar and a sash
that tied around the waist.

I wore it climbing trees,
digging graves for dead birds
and standing, properly attired,
as their solitary mourner.
I dripped fudgesicle on it

and the stain never showed.
I ran without impediment,
walked with a regal step, caught
lightning bugs in a glass jar,
skipped rope, swung so high
the chains nearly looped around

the bar, visited my grandmother
on Sunday afternoons. I wore
that dress until it was nothing
more than brown threads
and tattered edges, until my
mother brought home a yellow

dotted Swiss, two-piece bathing
suit with a ruffled bottom. I shifted
loyalty—wondered what the boy
next door would think of that.

Free Breakfast

The Springhill Suites free breakfast area
was filling up fast when a man carrying his
disabled young son, lowered him into his
chair, the same way an expert pilot's airplane
kisses the runway when it lands. And all the
while, the man whispered into his boy's ear,
perhaps telling him about the waffle maker
that was such a hit with the children gathered
around it, or sharing the family's plans for the
day as they traveled to wherever they were
going. Whatever was said, the boy's face was
alight with some anticipated happiness. And
the father, soon joined by the mother, seemed
intent on providing it. So beautiful they all
were, it was hard to concentrate on our eggs
and buttered toast, to look away when the
parents placed their hands on the little boy's
shoulders and smiled at one another, as if
they were the luckiest people in the room.

Goldfinch

for Felicia

Stunned by an unforgiving
pane of glass, a finch
fell to the ground
like a splash of pale
yellow paint. It sat
shivering in the snow,
its heartbeat faster
than a spinning bobbin
in the aftermath of such
a killing blow. Yet,
this little bird's thimble-
full of life held fast
to its fragile body,
and was soon cradled
by a loving human hand.
There, with splayed
feathers stroked smooth,
belly warmed by
a kind woman's skin,
the goldfinch rallied.
It spread its gilded wings
and flew to a snow-
laden branch, forgetting
before it got there,
the sky's unyielding
reflection—then flew
again—a bird-shaped
star with billions
of years left to burn.

Hospital Parking Lot

Headscarf fluttering in the wind,
stockings hanging loose on her vein-roped
legs, an old woman clings to her husband

as if he were the last tree standing in a storm,
though he is not the strong one.

His skin is translucent—more like a window
than a shade. Without a shirt and coat,

we could see his lungs swell and shrink,
his heart skip. But he has offered her his arm,
and for sixty years, she has taken it.

The Old Barn

So cold, you can see your breath in the old
barn, and sunlight slips through the narrow
spaces between slats. Spiders have looped
their sticky webs like makeshift curtains
around the dirt-smudged windows and the
air smells of cow dung and hay, both scents
hoof-stamped so deep into the floorboards,
nothing short of burning will get them out.
But it is peaceful here, among the ghosts
of livestock past, behind the house with its
caved-in roof and cramped, mouse-infested
rooms for which the word *abandoned* comes
to mind. But nothing says *defeat* in the barn.
It was built to last and it has lasted. Listen
and you will hear the echoes of well-fed cattle
lowing, the purr of a milk-whiskered barn cat,
the footsteps of a farmer's wife, the squeak
of her metal pail. The heart of this home was
here and it goes on beating when all else has
failed, when the money is gone and the family
has long since moved away. The fields may
be fallow, the ruts in the road beaten down by
cars that pass by rather than turn in, but the
barn remains, sturdy as the day it was raised,
doors open like a mother's welcoming arms.

Poem by a Woman with Glaucoma

Light is everywhere this morning—carried on the backs
of three songbirds flying past the pin oak tree, bouncing
off windows of the church behind our house, in a snail's

pearlized trail meandering around the patio. Dewdrops
look like sparkling diamonds strewn about the yard. And

on the floor of our screened-in porch, tiny flecks of mica
gleam like a thousand stars. Even the grille on a neighbor's
parked car is a miracle of light, and a lawn rake leaning

against a fence shines as though it were still in the store,
waiting to be bought. I want to press my face against the

sunlit panes in every room until light seeps into my cells,
until there is no darkness deep and wide enough to reach
me—and by this light, nothing in the world I cannot see.

Sheller

in memory of Mary Ann Eskridge

Though her skin has turned to rice paper,
her breathing shallow and sometimes labored,
she climbs the weathered stairs and crosses
the long boardwalk that leads to sand and sea.
At her back, the old lighthouse rises from the grassy
ground surrounding the Coast Guard station,
emitting every ten seconds, four one-second flashes
of light. And scattered across the dunes, sea oats
bob their blades to the crash of waves
while gulls wheel and cry above the sheller's bowed
head, her slight frame covered by a coat so heavy
she staggers at first, beneath its weight.
Yet she keeps going, buffeted left and right
by a chill wind, winding her way to where a thin
layer of shells—angel wings and Scotch
bonnets, pen shells and olives—rests near the shoreline.
And some days, if she's lucky, she finds a whole
sand dollar with its Star of Bethlehem
pattern, the five doves hidden within this delicate
disk released only after the shell is broken,
but she will not break it. She will carry
it home in her pocket, picturing all the while,
those unseen birds—their fragile wings spread
as if they are, already, in flight.

Stevie Santos

Stevie Santos wore his sister's slingbacks
to class, her false eyelashes. Silk shirts clung,
half-buttoned,

to his milk-white chest. Kids stared
and snickered, but Stevie's eyes faced forward,
like a soldier. With bombs of ridicule

exploding so close they might have blown him
to pieces, he marched down the pea-green
hallways of his father's alma mater,

painted toenails glittering. His step never
faltered—as if he saw clear through their jeering
faces to a tropical rainforest,

where birds with jeweled feathers called to one
another from the emerald trees—and nothing
on the ground could touch them.

Late Summer Blues

Summer has grown weary of itself.
It takes long naps among the cornstalks
in farmers' fields, each leaf sun-dried and as brittle
as dead bones—and in the corners of falling-down
shacks where rays of ever-thinning light shine
on abandoned webs and the empty husks of insects
that dangle from their threads. And when it wakes
summer scrawls its name on the dusty windows
of abandoned cars and squats by an old man changing
a tire by the freeway, blowing hot, dry air across
his weathered skin. It wanders down dirt roads
and gravel driveways, cement sidewalks
and woodland trails. Summer is anxious now
to be gone. It wants to loosen its grip on the brown
grass and yellow, ditch-growing flowers—
hitch a ride on the back of a broad-winged hawk
to places where the stars feel like chips of ice
sliding down September's throat.

Sorrow Bird

It feels as if my
face is not my

face anymore,

but an origami,
a sorrow bird

that flaps its

wings to no
avail—unable

to fly—a song

caught fast in
its paper throat.

To My Brother Who Died a Virgin

All you ever knew of naked women was that wet,
wadded-up magazine you and your buddies
found in a drainpipe. Their heads were thrown

back from their bare breasts like somebody socked
them in the jaw just before he took the pictures.

You never turned into your own driveway
the same time as your wife and kids—tumbled
through the door together and spent the evening

thinking how damn lucky you were, or the whole
night nestled so close to your wife's soft body a slip
of paper wouldn't fit between you. You never

woke up with tears of joy streaming down your face
from a dream that so resembled your real life,

you didn't realize you were sleeping. What you
got instead were the sounds of boys snickering—
sodden photographs of strangers who didn't love you.

ALTAIR

Laundry Day

On laundry day, they worked as a team. Trudging
up and down the basement stairs, my mother and
father took turns carting baskets of dirty clothes to
the washer and clean clothes from the dryer, doing
their best to avoid stepping on their ancient cat. She
liked to loll and stretch in front of the basement door
where sunlight from the kitchen fell just so across
the hallway floor, her body creating a trip hazard for
my father whose eyesight was slowly failing. Still,
Dad did his part which, over the years, changed to
folding rather than washing, at the insistence of my
mother. He would lift their dryer-warmed clothes,
crackling with static, and fold each piece with near
military precision—but also with tenderness when
it came to my mother's pants and shirts and gowns,
as if it were her skin he was touching, but could no
longer see. And she, in turn, took on the bulk of the
labor until washing clothes became less a chore and
more a ritual of love—one for the other—the two
of them as close on laundry day and every day, as
a pair of clean socks bound together in a drawer.

Bluebird

Light as crumbs on a plate,
a bluebird perched on the porch

railing, cocking its head this way
and that, feathers

the indigo blue of a king's hand-
dyed robe, or the sky

on its bluest day, drained of clouds
and concentrated in the bottom

of God's drinking glass, which He
swirled and swallowed,

then breathed out this little bird,
now flying.

The Ophthalmology Specialists' Secondary Waiting Room

Light is gentle here, and scarce—a room designed for dilated pupils, for patients with glaucoma, cataracts, and macular degeneration—people whose eyes have somehow failed them. Several wear dark sunglasses. Others blink and blot their eyes with tissues. At various times, every chair is taken. Then, a name is called, and after that, another. But no seat is vacant for long. There are so many of us, and so few hours left in the day. While we wait, some engage in whispered conversations. We compare eye pressures, past surgeries, and treatments, share stories like cowboys gathered around a circle of slowly dying embers—though most people sit in stoic silence, watching the wall-mounted TV, checking their cell phones, or staring into space. One elderly woman leans over her walker and shouts, *She*, pointing to her middle-aged daughter, *keeps shushing me*. And when her daughter says, with harried affection, *Shhh*, most can't help but smile, faces illuminated like priceless paintings by the faintest, yet unbearably beautiful, light.

Making the Biscuits

Wearing a plain cotton dress and work boots,
gray braids pinned to her head, my great-grandmother
bent down, scooped a palm-full of flour from a sack
on the floor, tossed it on the wooden block
beneath the window. Her hands, thick-knuckled,
arthritic—mixed, kneaded

and rolled wet dough as she stood in the narrow
pantry—a wall of shelves weighted with canned
vegetables on one side, dish towels drying
from a rope near the other. Flour rose

like puffs of smoke from her hands, floated
around her body in such profusion, it must have
seemed that she was fading from this world,
or had only just materialized from another.

By all accounts, she was a hard woman,
but Granny's biscuits were light as clouds—
soft in the center, crusty on top, perfect
for sopping up redeye gravy or Blackstrap

molasses. But first, she had to make them, day
after day, week after week, year after year—
before the sun rose over the distant trees, its face
round as the biscuit cutter she jabbed again
and again on the flour-dusted dough, her motions
quick as an adder, striking.

Girl with a Red Ribbon

inspired by "The Red Ribbon," by artist Abby Warman

This is not so much a girl standing on a sandy
beach, but the impression of a girl—

one who wears a white dress that is more
like a canvas upon which the rising sun paints

its roseate glow, its pale reflections of blue
water. She is carrying a straw hat and striped

towel. Tied in her hair is a bow the color of ripe
strawberries. Pausing in a pool of purple

meant to be her shadow, she is surrounded
by streaks of light as bright as an ivory gull's

feathers. Yet, it is the rich, red ribbon that calls
to women who remember well the pull

and tug of tying, our mother's hands as soft
as satin against the nape of our necks—how we,

impatient to be gone, barely felt them—would
give almost anything to feel them now.

The Referee

How long ago it seems when my middle-aged
father stood in our living room, practicing his
moves. He had a test to pass, signals to learn.
I sat on the couch, holding the local high school
football referee handbook, calling out words like:
delay of game, *pass interference*, and *personal
foul*. I would make up ways for him to memorize
motions, like naming one signal the *two-handled
teapot* and yet another, the *back off, buddy*. He
would work through the whole list after spending
eight hours at his day job. Still, I, a teenager who
had no knowledge of paying bills and feeding the
family, found it funny to see my father, once he
aced the test, wearing his new uniform—the stiff
white pants, his striped shirt, the shrill whistle that
hung around his neck. But I loved the hours we
spent together, laughing—how there was this thing
his daughter could do for him instead of the other
way around. Although I never saw my father on
the field, I can picture him there, his face lit by the
stadium lights as teams of fierce young men zoomed
back and forth across the yard lines, fans cheering
or jeering from the bleachers when Dad turned into
a two-handled teapot, full to the brim with fair play.

Frank and Alice: A Love Story

In the crowded confines of a noisy
newsroom, foreheads creased in concentration
over coffee-stained keyboards as story
after story was recorded, *clack, clack, clack*

with clerical precision. Phones cradled
on cricked shoulders fed "quotes"

to the eager ears of frenzied reporters
needing more substance to *flesh out* the skeletal
skittering of clipped sentences
glaring on their computer screens.

Fresh-faced, pencil-thin young women
snacked on fat-free yogurt and granola bars

while wrinkled old curmudgeons munched
three-day-old doughnuts.

And then there was Frank with his neat
containers of perfectly balanced meals, lovingly
prepared by his wife, whose nightly call
sent him into paroxysms

of astonished delight as if he never quite
believed his great good fortune of being the only
man in the whole world lucky enough
to marry Alice.

Pixie Cut

for my daughter

Black-eyed, black-haired girl of thirty-two,
I can see you reflected in a mirror
across the room—one of many mirrors and multiple stylists
with tattooed limbs and hennaed heads, clipping
and snipping. And I am thinking that the cloth draped
around your body, catching the sheared locks that tumble
to your shoulders, your lap, the floor, seems as sacred
as white linen on an altar table—your face emerging
like an angel sculpted from the clay
of your long, dark hair. You are smiling
because you see at last, what we all have seen—
how beautiful you are, that the woman you imagined
has arrived—
and she is and always has been, you.

Albino Opossum

Moon-marked, a bloated, bone-white marsupial
lay still in the road. No more lumbering through
the tall grass snout-first, its pale belly dragging

the ground like a choir boy's cassock. Solitary,
nomadic, and different since birth from its sisters
and brothers, this pallid possum stepped alone

onto the asphalt, claws clicking until it keeled
over as opossums will when frightened, and never
got up. There wasn't a mark on it from the metal

beast that barreled into its body, only a mound
of milky fur—its mouth, the pale pink of ballet
slippers, baring all fifty of its sharp little teeth.

Moon Walk

Sunburned, bellies full of fried pompano, sweet corn, and garden tomatoes purchased at a roadside stand manned by a farmer with more fingers than teeth—my family huddled around a rented black and white TV set the shape and size of a two-slot toaster, watching Neil Armstrong and Buzz Aldrin hop like bunnies on the rough surface of the same waxing moon that shone through our beach cottage windows. I was eleven years old, buck-toothed and long-legged—my brother a year younger and most days, followed his big sister like Mercury orbiting the sun. Mom and Dad sat side by side on the faux leather, sand-dusted couch and Grandma, never one to hold still for long, stood by her grandson's hard-backed chair, her hair a nimbus of silver from the soft glow of a television screen where a miracle unfolded before our eyes. But grown men wearing fishbowls on their heads, bouncing from one crater to the next, seemed less real to my brother and me than Saturday morning cartoons. And all the while, we could hear waves slapping the surf and wind whipping across the dunes—and the taste on every tongue was salt and more salt. So when I picture the summer of '69 at Long Beach, North Carolina, as history rolled out the red carpet leading to a future none of us could foresee, my heart breaks like an egg against the rim of what comes next. But let's pretend for the length of this poem, that my brother's blood remains safe inside his veins, Grandma's darkening mole as benign as a monastery full of monks, and our parents, unable to imagine the depth and breadth of grief. Here, there is only goodness and mercy, the light of a million stars, and the moon close enough now, for anyone to touch.

A Rancher Buries His Wife

They buried her in sunbaked ground, his wife
of fifty years.

A cowbird whistled from a crucifixion thorn,
and a freight train clacked

down the tracks. He stood apart
from the rest of them—folks whose names he

never cared to know, remembering of all things,
her hair haloed with light,

and the scent of her, still clinging to the clothes
she left behind.

He would die of it, this loneliness.
Already his hands were curling up, his fingers

turning blue. He used to be afraid of death.
Now he'd welcome it, like rain.

Stan's Place

When Irma worked the register, Stan relaxed. She'd sit, splay-legged, on a wooden stool, her stubby, beringed fingers as honest as the rest of her. No hair dye for Irma or fake femme fatale. She wore snap-front housecoats to work and a pair of mules. She smoked like a campfire and if customers complained, she gave them a look that made most people so jelly-legged and gut-twisted, they barely reached the restroom in time. For real troublemakers, Irma kept a custom-made pool cue at arm's length and she was lightning-fast at wielding it. Stan knew his money was safe with Irma, every penny accounted for at the end of her shift. They never talked about anything but business and that was okay by him. He didn't need to know more about Irma than he already knew, what with her little boy drowning all those years ago, in the creek behind her house. What some people carry, Stan often thought, shaking his head as Irma keyed in another six-pack, a lit cigarette dangling from her lips like a marker buoy bobbing above a wreck.

Sponge Bath

Draped in towels,
my grandmother sits in a hard-backed
chair, a white bowl

of soapy water on the floor.
She lifts her frail arm, then rests it,

gratefully, in her daughter's palm.
Gliding a wet

washcloth, my mother's hand
becomes a cloud, and every bruise, a rain-
drenched flower.

Slave Cemetery

Even as children, we sensed the slave cemetery
called for silence. We had no problem shouting
in the graveyard near our grandmother's house.
There, every plot was like a well-kept lawn—
the grass green and tender, the ground flat above
the graves as if there were no bodies buried beneath
the packed-down soil and strips of carefully laid
sod. Families filled brass urns with silk flowers—
jaunty bouquets dyed to match the season. Such
brilliant colors gave each site an air of celebration,
as if death were just a party we would all one day
attend—the markers like place cards on a fancy
dinner table. But in the slave cemetery, we couldn't
tell whose names were carved into the moss-covered
stones, cracked or crumbling. Some graves were
sunken as toothless faces. Others bore mounds
that looked freshly made, as if the dead could burst
free any moment, from dirt so loosely tamped on top
of their bones. And there was no grass or flowers,
only creeping vegetation that smelled of damp
and rot, bushes with thorns and trees with roots
so fat and twisted, they looked like anacondas
sleeping in the underbrush. In the slave cemetery,
death was tied forever to loss and sorrow, and we
were sorry. So we tiptoed around the tombs, quiet
as clouds. People buried here, deserve their rest.

A Nimble Deer

A doe that was, only a minute
before, quietly munching, leaps over
a wooden fence, nimble

as a goat. She rears up, after reaching
the other side, like a trick dog—
her front hooves dangling from her

useless forelegs, her hind legs
absorbing all the weight. She cranes
her soft, brown neck just far

enough to reach the succulent leaves
of a dogwood tree. But the younger
deer—smaller, less sure—

stick to low-hanging branches,
their tails flicking like little propellers
that fail to lift them from the earth.

New Bathing Suit

My friend is wearing her new black bathing suit.
It came with the proper cups, made to fill
with one breast and the memory
of another—which is not to say *emptiness*—
but the fullness that comes to us, with sacrifice.
There is no one more alive than she is now,
floating like a lotus or swimming, lap after lap,
parting the turquoise, chlorine-scented water,
her arms as sturdy as wooden paddles.
And when she pulls herself from the pool,
her new suit dripping—the pulse is so strong
in her wrists and throat, a little bird
outside the window will hear it, begin to flap
its wings to the beat of her heart.

ANTARES

The White Bench

High on a hill above our house, sits
a white, wrought iron bench that belonged
to my parents for years. It looks randomly placed,
as if it were lifted from their yard by a tornado,
and dropped where it is now, in mine.
But I can see it from our screened-in porch
and through all the back windows—the arched
backrest with its white roses and curled
leaves that almost look like lace, how it glows
and glistens when the sun begins to rise
above the red oaks and poplars. When resting
on its cool seat after climbing the steep hill,
I can see the whole neighborhood, as if I were a bird
on a branch. And the breeze seems to find me
there, on my parents' bench, more than
anywhere else in the yard—memories, too,
as well as scenes I can imagine—like my mother
spotting it in the store, how her face settled
into longing, how my father, who loved
her so, said *let's take it home*, and they did.

Ice Cream Truck

From blocks away we heard the mechanical
music the ice cream truck blared all over
the neighborhood, calling to kids like the Pied

Piper as we darted into our houses begging
our parents for change to buy Nutty Buddies

and banana popsicles, orange pushups
and ice cream sandwiches. Once the truck

stopped on our street, we swooped like seagulls
around the open window so the ice cream man
could take our money and hand out whatever

treats we asked for, which were always better
than we remembered from the last time his boxy,

hand-painted truck rolled around—the cold,
creamy confections freezing our tongues and

sliding down our parched throats as fast as we
could eat them—the taste of summer lingering
just long enough to make us wish for more.

Kenmore

The Kenmore range tried to make friends
with the other appliances, but the refrigerator
gave her the cold shoulder. Besides, he hummed
all the time and his breath smelled like moldy
cheese. The microwave made her jump when
he said *ding*, and his face was always dirty—
smeared with exploded eggs and bits of hotdog.
The can opener poked her nose into everybody's
business and the toaster had a crummy personality,
so making friends with them was out. That left
the dishwasher, who foamed at the mouth like
a rabid dog whenever he cleaned the dishes.
She wished the washing machine and dryer—
such a nice, quiet couple—lived closer, but they
were in the basement, a dark, dank place the owner
hardly ever visited. He seldom cooked a real meal,
either, so the range sat idle, mourning the house
from where she was recently removed, making
way for the newest model. She tried winking
all four of her eyes at the lonely man who bought
her, but he never noticed—just microwaved
his dinner and took it into the den. She missed
listening to people talk around a kitchen table;
pined for boiling pots and moo-cow oven mitts;
remembered all too well how good her belly felt
when it was full of turkey and rump roast, pork
loin and Cornish hens. Once, she felt needed,
necessary, part of a family. Now she's just
an old stove, cool to the touch, with nothing
but memories to keep her warm.

County Fair

Pulled like rotten teeth from the open mouths
of mineshafts, massive pyramids of gleaming
coal dot the landscape of Kanawha County.
Coal dust fine and black as pulverized midnight,
covers everything for miles. Rows of ramshackle
houses kneel by the river like washer women
with their knees in river muck, and jagged
mountains cut the slate-gray sky

to ribbons. But the Kanawha River is long
and winding, and leads to a lone Ferris wheel
rising up from the bottomland, jaunty
as an Easter bonnet. Its rainbow-colored gondolas
call to mind a different tune than the dismal dirges
of Black Lung and White Damp. They carry the sound
of children's laughter through the ground
and into the mines, like light.

Gardening Lesson

At the end of our backyard by an old metal
fence that had long since collapsed like a weary
runner after crossing the finish line, Granddaddy
picked up a shovel and stuck it into the rigid
earth that did not easily yield to his digging.
My brother and I, still small children, watched
him work—noted the beads of sweat gathering
on his broad forehead and soaking through his
cotton shirt. His black hair, slick with tonic,
gleamed in the hot sun, and his glasses kept
slipping down his nose. It took a while for him
to dig a big enough patch of ground and divide
it into neat rows, where the packets of seeds
we held in our hands would soon be scattered.
Peas, carrots, and squash—nothing my brother
and I liked to eat if we were honest, were our
grandfather's vegetables of choice, though we
could not imagine such tiny seeds turning into
the same stuff we pushed around our plates at
dinner time, most often hiding them under the
mashed potatoes. But we dutifully shook them
out and tamped down the ground, while Grand-
daddy grabbed the hose and watered a garden
we hoped would take a hundred years to grow.

Brilliant Delusion

There is something magical about lamps
on a screened-in porch,
the amber glow beneath a hand-sewn
shade, the graceful flare

of fabric directing the beams. Lamps
illuminate this human foray
into the outdoors when other creatures
must rely on the mercurial

moon. Secure in our protective illusion
of mesh, we enjoy the night air

without the bother of insects. We lock
the flimsy door against intruders,
creating a chimera of security. Yet it
is the light more than anything else,

like campfires dotting the open plains,
that quiets our fears. Perhaps animals

are smarter, understanding that nothing
holds back the darkness of deadly

intent. They crouch in the bushes
and hide in the trees while we play cards
and laugh out loud, pretending we
are invincible in our radiant cocoons.

Loving You Burns Like Shingles

My love for you is a sun inside my chest.
It burns like shingles, wrings tears from my eyes
like the hands of a tough old woman washing
clothes in a tin tub. You're as toxic as poke salad,
your words a swarm of bees. You haunt me
like a chain-clanking ghost, yet I welcome you
like the mailman. You're a zeppelin in disguise,
the zip line to disaster. I need you like bad brakes,
a stick of dynamite, loose bricks in the walk.
But step into a room and my heart bumps its mouth
against the bowl of my ribs like a starving
goldfish. You scissor-cut my will, turn my brain
to shredded wheat. Look at me once, and my pot
begins to boil. Look at me twice, and the dog
of my desire becomes a junkyard beast—
though the feral cat in me hungers
to call your body *home*.

Soleá

a tribute to flamenco dancer Soledad Barrio

Salome's dance started with seven veils, but Soledad
Barrio, fully clothed, is naked beneath the spotlight.
From the moment she appears whatever

is not this woman, this stage, this *cantaor's* plaintive
voice, the *palmeros* clapping, the intricate riffs
on the guitar—no longer matters.

Mesmerized first by her face, we watch her hypnotic
hands begin to undulate like sea anemones,
her supple, sensuous body telling a thousand tales

of passion and pain, rage and exile, her feet pounding
the floor like a barrage of cannon fire as she inhales,
exhales, her lungs working like a bellows.

She is magnificent and haunting, the embodiment
of *duende* as she dances like a Rom around a bonfire,
as if her life is a flame that will soon burn out.

Even Soledad's shadow is alive, pulsing with its own
beating heart, her body like a vein thick with heat
and blood until the final *braceo*—

her arms extended like the limbs of a twisted tree,
reaching beyond the limits of muscle, skin, and bone—
the stage hot enough now, to birth a star.

Nighthawks

What became of the middle-aged men wearing suits, ties, and fedoras, who once frequented the counters of cheap downtown diners late at night, nursing cups of black coffee and the last pieces of blueberry pie?

Where did they go? Perhaps heaven is, for them, like an Edward Hopper painting—with people sitting in diners, bathed in artificial light, keeping themselves

to themselves. There might be other customers there whom they don't know. And one is probably a pretty redhead—nice to look at but there's no need for any

strained conversation—and just the right guy behind the counter who keeps the hot coffee coming and his mouth shut. It doesn't matter that the shops across the

street are dark, and nobody's strolling past. There will always be light to see by, but nothing we see of them save the cut of their clothes and their cambered backs as they lean over eternity—well-lit and forever alone.

Fog

Beyond a grass-covered hill as yellow
as nicotine-stained fingers, fog rises like smoke
swirling around the trunks and naked limbs

of the poplar trees. A pair of hawks cry out
to one another, and chickadees scatter,
their small bodies lighter than the sodden air.

All morning long, this fog has lingered
like it will never lift, as though some benevolent
god has softened forever, the world's sharp

edges. Deer have merged with the woods, birds
with branches, mice with the fields—as fog
moves across winter-weary lands

like a stampede of silent, silver-coated horses,
the sound of their hoof beats muffled
by muddy ground. Yet, above our sheltering

roofs, the sun is hiding behind a wall of clouds,
and all around it, invisible stars still shine.
So let the fog go on dangling like lace

from the pearl-gray sky, blurring and blending
the miles between us—until there is nothing
left of missing you, but the taste of rain.

Hate Crime

To the teenager who tackled the Asian American
taking out his garbage, who screamed
the words, *kung flu*, spittle flying
from your crooked mouth: Last night the old man
you punched in the face again and again,
turned eighty-four. His great-granddaughter,
aged nine, wrote a birthday poem. She read it to him
from her pink bedroom while he sat in his kitchen,
a thousand miles away. He had never been so happy,
even as a boy. Today, his glasses are broken,
his elbows and knees bloody. There are holes
in his carefully creased trousers, his good
jacket. You never looked back, just kept walking
down the street where the old man lived
for forty years, as if the sidewalk belonged to you—
while the father, grandfather, great-grandfather
you left lying on the ground, watched through
swollen eyes, a pair of clouds float
across the sky like swans.

Rain

Rain is made of whispers
and sighs, the exhalation
of heavenly creatures

who peer at us from the
clouds. Each droplet
makes its way from the sky,

leaping like an acrobat
in silver leotards, landing
nimbly and gracefully

on leaves and blossoms
and the upturned faces
of little children who have

no makeup to run or hairdos
to ruin. It pools in low-
lying places, with colors

gathering at the edges
in rainbow hues; it sinks
into the ground, nourishing

plants and tiny insects
whose thirst exceeds their
fear of drowning.

It is music for lovers,
a lullaby for babies cozy
in their cradles. Rain

strokes the earth until it
resembles an Impressionist
painting, until it gives

way its indurate shell and
lies open—becomes as soft
as a newborn's palm.

At the Poultry Show

My dad, wearing a Cattleman hat, Western belt, and
Levi jeans, strode in his pointy, hand-tooled leather
boots toward the prize-winning poultry, his favorite

fair exhibition. He loved them all: Wyandottes, Rose-
comb Bantums, Buckeyes, Australorps, and the rest,

stopping by every cage to give the best their due. He
listened to their clucks and crows as if he and they

were engaged in serious conversation. He watched
them strut and shake their fiery combs, compared

their wattles to his own. Wild about the Rainbow
Roosters, Silver-Laced Polish, and Showgirl Silkies,

my father would linger a bit longer to marvel at their
magnificent plumage before moving on to the next.

And when at last he exited the building, Dad would
stand for a moment, squinting in the sun, and pick
stray feathers from his shirt like a rooster, preening.

The Physics of Fishing

Bobby keeps his guns close and his dog
closer. He has a PhD in physics, so his buddies
down at the local bar like to hear about stuff

he knows, like space is restless and wind casts
a shadow. But mostly, Bobby likes to drink
alone in his own basement with a wood fire

burning and trees shaking like palsied old
men around his house. His dog, Albert
Einstein, loves to lay his gray muzzle in his

master's lap and dream of younger days,
when running was easy and his mouth knew
the shape of a dead squirrel's body better

than his own teeth. Still, he and Bobby
would go fishing come morning, for salmon
running upstream while dodging hordes

of hungry brown bears. And whatever they
caught would be tomorrow night's supper,
along with cornbread baked in an iron

skillet. It is a good life and as simple as Bobby
can make it—as far from a city and as close
to the Kenai River as he could get, although

he knows nothing truly touches anything else
the way most everybody thinks, not a hook
and a fish, or even a man and his dog.

The Peony

A single peony,
the pale pink
of a young
girl's flushed
cheek, sits in
a slender glass
vase. Water
droplets tremble
on its petals.
A few slip
silently to the
polished table,
while others
remain, holding
on to the light.

After the Explosion

My brother, splayed on the concrete like a bearskin rug, body broken, eyes filmy, died in a river of red that flowed as if the summer air were a vampire, crazed with hunger. It ran in rivulets down the driveway, into a street lined with neighbors upon whose retinas the image of his death was burned. Perhaps his spirit lingered for a while, leery of its new and borderless dimensions—entered a tool lying on the garage floor, marveling at the chill of his cold, metal skin. Next, the bee flying over the heads of paramedics frantically working, the buzz like nothing he ever felt, a rumbling deep in his chest, the clap of wings much softer than hands. And after that, a few more stops— the cement statue of the shy girl our mother bought for the garden, the dog next door that wouldn't stop barking, the taste of its pink tongue strange and wild in a mouth that opened wider than any door. And out of that dog's mouth my brother shot into the sky like a bottle rocket, though none of us looked up. How I wish we could have seen his swift ascent, the pressures of his life: go to school, get a job, conform, conform, conform—lift like a piano from his chest, his soul rising weightless, without impediment, until he reached the stars from which we all are made and zoomed by them, faster than any plane he dreamed as a boy, to fly.

VEGA

Breakfast with My Parents

I loved my parents' pillow-creased faces,
their soft robes—how their house smelled
of fresh-perked coffee, orange juice, and
toast with strawberry jam. We would sit
together at the table, my mother slicing
and sugaring my father's grapefruit since
he could hardly see it—my father holding
a newspaper his failing eyesight no longer
let him read. Still, he liked the feel of it in
his hands, the sound of the paper rustling.
He would eat the glistening pieces of fruit,
talking between bites, his voice deep and
gravelly in the mornings. Then my mother
would scramble a few eggs with a whisk,
add a dash of cold milk, a shake or two of
black pepper. While waiting for his eggs
to cook, Dad sometimes turned on his old
radio, where cheerful voices said what he
already knew. It would be a perfect day.

Bare Tree in the Afternoon

after a painting by Clyde Edgerton

You can tell a storm is coming by the dark clouds
gathering like a herd of gray sheep. Still,
there is a bit of blue left in the sky and the sun

is casting its golden light on the bare tree
and grassy ground. Yellow as daffodils, sunlight
clings to the tree's bark and its slender

branches as it flecks, streaks, and dapples the steep,
green hillside. Ruts in the nearby road suggest
a traveler motoring by—perhaps hurrying

home to beat the rain. But the clouds have not yet
emptied their silver buckets, nor has light
ceded its bright dominion over the landscape.

That tranquil moment between what might happen
and what will, has been thoroughly captured.
The artist is asking the viewer

to open the mind's umbrella and then to cast it
aside—to see the dark and threatening sky
as simply a backdrop for everything that shines.

The Doctor Who Dies of the Coronavirus After the Hospital Runs Out of Gloves

There is no linear time in the hereafter. Angels do everything at once. They see the last pair of latex gloves drop to a hospital floor in slow motion, the look of fear on the face of the gloveless doctor who, in the blink of a human eye, goes on caring for patients. They can watch people being brave (since fear is the birthplace of bravery) and the people who are sick, some of them dying. But those who pass away during the doctor's glove-free hours feel the touch of warm skin on his or her forehead when they take their final breaths. This is the unselfish mercy that humans are capable of, which makes the angels marvel. Divine creatures respect mortality and all that it entails. And from every angel's non-linear, eternal perspective, a doctor can do his job, and at the exact same time enter the great mystery of his own dying. Angels may ooh and ahh over this lone human being's merciful acts as well as mercy shown around the world, and still catch his soul the instant it leaves his body. One whispers words of solace. Yet another sings the doctor's favorite aria, Puccini's "O Mio Babbino Caro," as they carry him to the place where there is no grief or sorrow—and no need for gloves at all.

Empathy

Close as two women crooning into the same
microphone, they sing their sorrows
to one another in a grocery store parking lot,

keys dangling from their hands, cars waiting
still and silent as good dogs, beside them.

People pass by unnoticed; the sky grows dark.
On and on they stand, rooted to the pavement—

sharing sadness like a loaf of warm bread—
eyes luminous as pearls formed by her friend's

suffering. Perhaps the stars will wish on them
tonight. For even as they part, briefly

touching, their glow is brighter—the ground
lit beneath their feet as they walk away,
each wearing the other woman's shoes.

Angel

I used to see them walking, a middle-aged
man and his grown son, both wearing brown
trousers and white shirts like boys in a club,
or guys who like to simplify. But anyone
could see the son would never be a man who
walked without a hand to hold, a voice telling
him what to do. So the father held his son's
hand and whispered whatever it was the boy
needed to know, in tones so soft and low it
might have been the sound of wings pressing
together again and again. Maybe it was that
sound, since the father had the look of an angel
about him, or what we imagine angels should
be—a bit solemn-faced, with eyes that view
the world through a lens of kindness—who
sees every man's son as beautiful and whole.

Sunrise Avenue

Take me back to Sunrise Avenue
in the Chihuahuan Desert with its cadmium-yellow
light and miles of sand punctured by prickly

pear cactus, ocotillo, and Texas rangers with their
purple blooms. Here, our mother is wearing
a quilted robe and having breakfast

with our father. My brother and I, already dressed,
can hardly wait to run out the front door
of our small apartment not far from where a row

of rugged mountains looms like the bodies
of armor-plated dinosaurs, still sleeping.
But the sun is pressing its fiery face against the sky's

cool, blue window, and the day has begun. I will push
my doll's stroller around the sandblasted
parking lot with my brother trailing

after me—watch our mother swoon in our father's
arms before he leaves for work. Let me
have again, if only for an hour, everything I have lost.

Estaleen

The first time fifteen-year-old Jay saw eighteen-year-old Estaleen Renee Porter, who haunted his dreams for the rest of his life, she was standing in the driveway outside his grandmother's beauty shop, flicking ashes from a Pall Mall smoked down to a nub, into an empty bottle of Fresca. *Hey there*, she said, and he said, *Hey*, just like a parrot, he thought to himself, looking for a cracker. So, when the door to the beauty shop swung open and his grandmother shouted, *Jaybird, you get on in here and help Nana with Grandmaw Porter's permanent*, Jay was both relieved and humiliated. His grandmother was the worst hairdresser in town since she had no training and opened the shop because she was bored after retiring from the phone company, and Papaw left her what she referred to as his *nest egg* when he drowned in the dog's water bowl. How he passed out face-down in that precise spot remains an unsolved mystery, yet it definitely wasn't suicide so the life insurance people had to pay up, too. But as bad as Nana was at cutting hair, her inability to properly mix the ingredients for dye jobs and perms had already rendered at least a dozen customers as bald as the day they were born. She had her regulars all the same because she was cheaper than anybody else and a good listener. And when her grandson stayed with her for a week or two in the summer, he did all the mixing and she usually got much better results. Still swooning, however, from his first glimpse of the most beautiful girl he'd ever seen outside a movie theater, Jay mixed a little too much of this and not enough of that, and half of Miz Porter's curls fell out on the way home, the shock causing Estaleen to crash her 1955 Dodge Dart into a water hydrant, which launched her singing career in Nashville when a record producer in town to visit his older brother heard her melodic cries for help as she dragged her unharmed, partially bald, hysterical grandparent from the twisted wreckage and he signed Estaleen Renee to her first record deal on the spot.

Heaven

You wake in a sun-drenched room
with knotty pine walls and open windows,

white curtains billowing. The warm,
salt-scented breeze carries

the sound of waves, the laughter of children,
the cry of gulls. Somewhere

inside the house, bacon sizzles in a pan,
coffee drips in a pot—and there are voices,

familiar voices—your grandmother,
your brother, your best friend. It's been

so long since you have seen them.
So you sit up in bed, stretch your strong,

supple limbs. There is no pain,
no stiff shoulders and creaky joints.

There is no weight of sorrow or regret—
only a kind of soaring joy that lifts

and circles inside you like a kite.
And when you move across the floor,

it feels like floating, as if your body is made
of light and air—but solid when

they reach for you, when their arms
open wide and you walk in.

Sugar

Give me some sugar, people used
to say to get a good-bye kiss. But sugar
is bad for you now and crossed

off our list. It only leads to weight
gain and inflammation, not to
mention condemnation from those

whose idea of a *treat* is eating one
more sprout or an extra beet. Without
sweets I would be thinner and no

doubt a little healthier. Most definitely,
I would be wealthier. But what good
is supper without a sugar upper—

chocolate chip cookies, layer cakes,
eclairs and cinnamon rolls, dollops
of homemade ice cream melting

in bowls? If I'd been Eve, the world
would not have fallen. I only eat
apples in pie or stollen.

Papa's Chair

I picture my great-grandfather's strong,
woodworking, beekeeping, ground-tilling,
coffin-making, baptizing, Bible-holding
hands resting on the rounded ends of his
chair's solid walnut arms, his slender body
light against an upholstered seat that never
sagged beneath his weight. No sharp edges
here, only graceful curves and smooth arches—
narrow at the back, wide at the front—like
a woman whose child will soon be born. Its
legs are sturdy, too, like Papa's were from
miles of walking—its feet securely planted
behind the pulpit in the little country church
where Papa preached. I imagine him sitting
there, waiting, going over in his mind what
he wanted to say to the congregation, his
sharp eyes bluer than a summer sky, his hair
as black as words on printed pages he never
learned to read. Now, Papa's chair—which
so often held in its arms, a man whose kind-
ness seeped into the wood like linseed oil—
is so close to me as I write these lines, it is
like his hand is on my shoulder and Papa is
preaching just for me, about everlasting love.

Thread Count

My mother hung wet sheets to dry from a rope
that stretched between two poles in our backyard,
her motions smooth and rhythmic as a synchronized
swimmer. She stooped and straightened again
and again, her hands moving across the line faster
than squirrels on telephone wire.

From my perch on the swing, I watched her work,
pumping my legs until I touched puffy
white clouds with the toes of my shoes, the squeak

of the metal chain steady as a metronome.
My body felt light as dandelion seeds, floating.
Higher and higher I swung, until it seemed
I was a kite soaring on the end

of a string. I slung my head back and let my hair
trail in the dirt, closing my eyes so the sensation
in my belly was like the swift

descent of an elevator in a tall building. The sun
felt like warm maple syrup dripping
on my face, and the air smelled of honeysuckle
and bacon grease in glass jars sitting on the window
sill. I opened my eyes as my mother lifted
the last sheet from the pile, with light illuminating
the threads like the hours in a child's summer day,
too many to count.

Betty's Roadside Diner

Unaware of its anachronistic status,
Betty's Roadside Diner with its rusty sign blinking,
stands between mile markers
on a desert highway. Like a blazing

campfire to a cluster of tired cowpokes, the diner,
with its dazzling lights, lures
lonely drifters and famished families,
road-weary truckers and the down
and out. You can still get a piece of fruit pie
for a dollar fifty and free re-fills
on coffee, and somebody's

sure to say hello when you walk in.
The waitresses look like sisters, with lined
faces and chiseled cheekbones,
their hair (the color of mud flats

or dust bunnies) laminated with generous
layers of hairspray. They wait patiently,
(holding tiny lead pencils), to write
down your culinary pleasure
while the greasy air coats

your lungs slick as corn oil
in a cast-iron skillet. The fry-cook scrapes
a metal spatula over an open griddle,

dividing heaping mounds of hash brown
potatoes into separate servings
and scooping them into plates

that rattle on the countertop every time
a big rig rumbles by.

Florescent tubes that line
the ceiling are so bright, you can see your own
soul through the backs of your hands,
(though it doesn't seem to bother babies,

curled in corner booths like cocktail shrimps,
dreaming the night away). There's a sense
of isolation surrounding everyone,

as if they're actors in separate plays—
yet it comforts you to see them. In fact,

it seems like all that's warm and safe
in the whole world lies amid the fake-leather seats
and unfamiliar faces of folks who wound
up here tonight, in the same place as you.

Bloom

She is alone, save for the cat curled
around her feet, its fur thick as the winter
coat of a brown bear sleeping in its cave. The chill
wind roars through the woods like something dangerous—
yet tonight, she is warm and safe. Funny how cancer is silent,
like dark clouds floating over a field. Left unchecked,
it goes on doing its work—as if a body
is a house that needs tearing down, a place where no one wants to live
anymore. But she isn't done with her body, her life.
The ground may be frozen, but spring
will come again for her, the cat, the sleeping bears,
the birdsfoot violets, and the great blue heron
she saw last year along the Creeper Trail. The cup of tea
steaming in her hands will turn to lemonade
with shaved ice, and light will fall just so through the leaves,
the branches, calling to everything alive: bloom.

Lightning Bugs

Lightning bugs—little sparks from the earth's
fiery core, dusk's tiny lanterns—by their light,
I can see my childhood. I run barefoot again
through new-mown grass, my hair wild and

tangled as old fishing nets, the bulbs on those
blinking bodies leading us into our neighbors'
yards and down the sidewalk to the tune

of the streetlights' hum. Parents sit in semi-
circles on one another's front lawns, drinking
lemonade from Dixie cups and the occasional

Tom Collins until it grows dark and the time
comes to call their children in for baths and bed.
Then glass jars filled with dozens of flickering
bugs will flash yellow and green from night-

stands in a neighborhood where we fall asleep
in seconds, believing summer days will always
end like this one—our skin still glowing from
all the light we have gathered in our hands.

Portrait of Elizabeth

for Diana

Standing on a windswept beach
with the warm sun shining on
her upturned face and lithe,
long-legged body, my friend's
lovely daughter is the epitome
of bliss. With her arms flung back
behind her shoulders, eyes closed,
she is smiling as if the new day
is a carnival ride and she is happy
to be on it. The pool of water
shimmering beneath her bare
feet, the azure sea and its frothy
waves forever curling, the milky-
blue sky, are the perfect settings
for this jeweled moment in time,
where grief and loss are nowhere
to be found—only joy, only joy.

At the Drive-In

You parked your father's car in this very field
and hurried to the concession stand, dodging fireflies
and wayward children running from their mothers.

As you stood in line, you glanced over your shoulder
at the yellow-haired girl whose hands rested in her lap

like fresh-picked lilies, who smiled at you like you were
someone she'd been waiting for all her life; except you
didn't think such things back then. You only knew that she

was with you voluntarily, which seemed to you a miracle—
and if you managed not to spill your drink on her dress
or snag her lip with your braces, she might let you touch

some small part of her skin, however briefly. So you
slid in beside her, fixed the speaker to the window. You
watched the actors move and speak and play out their

scripted lives on the whitewashed shingles of a makeshift
movie screen, but what you remember most are the stars

that twinkled all around it, and how her hair felt soft
as leaves brushing against your cheek. And even now,
years later, the concession stand closed, the ticket booth

locked—the screen fallen to its wooden knees in the tall
grass—the stars still twinkle above the abandoned
field, and the old man gazing up at them, smiling.

ARCTURUS

Washing Dishes

Side by side my parents stand at the old double
sink, doing the dishes from their supper. You
can see them through the kitchen window, Mom
washing, Dad drying, their faces glowing like
incandescent bulbs. My mother dips a dirty glass
in the warm, sudsy water, soaps it clean, and rinses
it off. Then she passes it to my father, who has
so little feeling in his knotty fingers a glass could
be a bubble for all he knows. Still, he manages
to hold it. He rubs its slippery surface with the
dishcloth and sets it in the drainer, then reaches
for a dinner plate and does the same. One by one,
they wash and dry them, every glass and plate
and bowl and pot until the counter is bare, all the
while talking the way people do when they've
known each other so long, you'd think there was
nothing left to say. Yet for them, conversation
never ends. It is the music of my childhood, my
parents' voices—a comforting cadence to anyone
close enough to hear them sing to one another
night after night, their sweet dishwashing song.

Red Tractor

Just before you reach the Triple B Country
Sausage sign, there's an old red tractor
hunkering down beside the road.

You can hear the heavy sighs as it nestles
into the leaves, loosening its belt
and letting its chassis hang low. Blink

and you'll miss it twitch like a sleeping dog—
the rise and fall of its rust-covered ribs
when it rolls at last, into a dream of wheat.

At the Cosmetic Counter

You should have seen my mother
just before she stepped out the door
for work. She wore a crisp white
lab coat with silver buttons, the
letter "C" for Clinique pinned near
the lapel. Her long hair was like
a shadow on a field of snow as she
swept through the house, searching
for her purse and keys to the old
station wagon that never failed
to bring her home. We took it all
for granted, my brother and I, when
wiping *Bronze Leaf* lipstick from
our cheeks after she kissed us both
good-bye—assumed she would
always come back, that mothers
never age or die. We carried on
with our teenage lives while hour
after hour, she held other women's
faces in her hands—each customer
walking out looking better than
when she walked in. It wasn't just
the makeup, lotions, and creams,
but the gentleness with which they
were applied—how our mother, with
her flawless skin and *Bronze Leaf*
smile, made them feel so beautiful.

Autumnal Equinox

There is some sense when autumn
begins, that the world
is being smothered by a colorful
blanket. Trees lose
their emerald radiance. The edges
of their leaves turn yellow,
orange, or scarlet. Days grow
shorter and shadows linger. Nights
come with a chill like bathwater
left in the tub too long. Flowers,
that bloomed in lush profusion
on my front porch, droop

like tired children fighting sleep.
Vidalia onions and garden tomatoes
disappear from grocery store
shelves, replaced by pumpkins
and oddly shaped squash.

When autumn arrives, winter
is only a frozen breath away,
bringing cold and slush, runny noses
and hacking coughs, gray
mornings and twilight afternoons.

It is the season that swallows
summer like it never was—
as if young girls in sundresses
were never kissed in the moonlight,
and baseballs never soared over
a fence. There were no barbecues
or mosquito bites, sandals filled
with sand on the deck.
Autumn shakes the summer
from our minds until it falls
like leaves skittering down
an empty street.

Sabine LeBlanc

Sabine LeBlanc liked bourbon balls
and deer meat chili, air so hot and
sticky, insects caught fire in the air,
but never fell. The power in her row
house went out at least once a week
when a hard rain let loose from the sky
like fenced-in bulls, flattened ant hills
and pounded the hides of big gators
lying as still as wooden planks in the
shallow water of the bayou. Stray dogs
wallowed in the mud and half-naked
kids splashed through water pooling
in the street. Her next-door neighbors,
an elderly pair named Alphonse and
Henri, liked to sit on their porch, rain
or shine, smoking King Edward cigars
and hollering *Bonjou* to the passersby.
And Monday mornings, Sabine's long-
time lover played smooth jazz on his
sax while she pinned up her hair for
work and painted her lips, still swollen
from kisses, as red as a cayenne pepper.

Tomato Sandwich

Leaning on the counter
by an open window
with tomato juice dripping down
your chin and mayonnaise
gathering

in the corners of your mouth
as soggy, white bread
sticks to your teeth

and your tongue tingles

from the tangy taste of salt
and pellets of fresh
ground pepper burn the back

of your throat, you can't help
but think that eating
a garden tomato sandwich
in your own kitchen is finer
than a café lunch
in Paris.

Sundays

Sunday school was alright with its cups
of orange juice and Lorna Doone cookies.
And Jesus sounded like a nice guy, if
a little obsessed with sheep. But the fun
really started when our mother shed
her Sunday clothes and slung her high-
heeled shoes into the closet, and Daddy,
who pulled off his tie before we even
reached the car, turned on the TV and
settled into his chair with a sigh so deep,
it seemed like the earth trembled from
the force of his relief. Then Mama, still
wearing her silky white slip, her bare feet
slapping the cool kitchen floor to the
sound of Betty Everett singing "The Shoop
Shoop Song," fried chicken so light and
crispy, it nearly floated off our plates.
To us, death was nothing but a fly stuck
to a swatter. And sickness meant sore
throats, or a stomachache soothed by
a dose of Paregoric. We didn't know
we needed to hold on tight to Sundays—
make them last as long as anything that
melts can ever last—leaving our hands
as empty as a room once a party's over,
the people all gone, and the lights out.

My Father's Cowboy Boots

My father's cowboy boots
will never again

be parted. They sit side
by side like old

men on a park bench who
have been friends so

long, there is nothing left
for them to say.

Alvin and Ila

In this old photograph, it is summertime and my grandparents, Alvin and Ila, are sitting in lawn chairs by their house on Martin Street. My grandmother is taking a sip of coffee, her head bowed as if in prayer. Her gray hair is combed away from her forehead, her skin as smooth as her cup. She is wearing a light blouse with a floral pattern that flatters her petite figure, her small waist. My grandfather's face is in profile, his dark hair gleaming in the sun. His body has thickened in late middle age, so he is barrel-chested in his white dress shirt, and heavy of jowl. But his hand, holding his lit cigarette, is the same hand that held his bride so tenderly as they stood, pressed together on a riverbank, kissing with such abandon that the person who captured it on film must have felt like an intruder. But in this picture, taken decades later, no part of their bodies is touching, though their chairs are side-by-side, and their right legs crossed in the same direction. Ila's toes are curled in the slipper-soft shoes she liked to wear, and Alvin's black leather shoe follows the arc of his wife's narrow foot. They are as close as a pair of ice skaters, perfectly aligned, just before they join hands and glide away.

Wisteria

Indolent flowers, how
firmly your vines
wrap around a host,

like the arms of a jewel
thief and a woman

wearing diamonds.
Your divine sense
of color, your heady

scent, are powerful
arguments for survival.

You fall like clusters
of grapes, your petals
both heavy and delicate,

like Sumo wrestlers
drinking tea from

porcelain cups. You are
the perfect distraction
as your stem and roots

work their way into,
around, between,

and over everything
in sight, like cool green
lava with lavender ashes.

Egg Salad

I make it like my mother did. Boil the eggs.
Let them sit awhile in a pot of cold water.
Then I peel them on a paper plate, wash stray

bits of shell from my fingers. I use a fork to
mash the whites and yolks, add mayonnaise
and yellow mustard—a splash of apple cider

vinegar, salt, and pepper. Then I spread the egg
salad on soft, white bread, cut my sandwiches
into quarters like my mother did when I was

small. I can almost see her hands, seldom still,
peeling and washing, preparing and slicing,
each motion swift and sure. It was my mother's

hands, when they laid her body out for a final
viewing—as fixed as a pair of songbirds fallen
from the sky—that convinced me she is gone.

Shrimp Boat Captain

The craggy-faced shrimp boat captain
keeps a pinch of chewing tobacco between
his lip and gum, wears faded blue overalls
and a ball cap. Early mornings, you'll
find him lumbering down the road towards
an old wooden pier, carrying a cooler filled
with ice, a fishing rod slung over his beefy
shoulder. Tackle swings like a pendulum
behind his back until he reaches his favorite
bench, close to the end. He pulls a bag
of shrimp from the cooler, baits his hooks
and casts his line as far as arthritis allows—
sits there until noon, either catching fish
or not; it's all the same to him. It's the sun
and wind and rain he's come for—the view
of shrimp boats headed out to sea, crews
tiny as toy soldiers. He can hear the cries
of hungry gulls, feel each vessel's pitch
and toss, though he is captain of nothing
now, save his own soul. And what his soul
wants is to keep his body close to water—
until the moon captures him in her net and lifts
it with cool, white hands into the starry sky.

Cling Peaches

I'm sitting by your hospital bed
The morning after we almost lost you—
Feeding you canned peaches with
A plastic spoon. You seldom speak,
With cancer ravaging your fine
Mind like a plague of hungry locusts,
But you seem more yourself today
Than you have in weeks. Your
Gaze is tender as a bruise, and my
Hand trembles, lifting the spoon
To your mouth. Your recent rousing
Performance of *Husband, Dying*,
Has ripped the rose-colored glasses
Right off my face. You aren't going
To get well, after all, despite our
Murmured prayers and midnight
Promises to be good forever, if only.
How like you, though, to hold
A dress rehearsal—eyes shut, your
Leonine head crushing the pillow,
Sheets bunched like drifts of
Snow covering your too-still body.
It became real for me then, your
Death. I wanted to tie you
To the bedrails, stand guard with
A flaming sword, daring anyone,
Anything, to try and take you.
Instead, I feed you cling peaches,
Letting go of you a little more,
My darling, with every bite.

In the Midst of Grief, a Heron

Healing begins with the blue heron hunting
in the frigid water of a shallow pond.

Wings folded, neck tucked into its feathered
breast, it stands motionless in a shelter

made of branches, alone save for its shadow.
What would it hurt to loosen our grip

on grief? To allow the soft gray-blue
of a heron's body to soothe our eyes, tired

of shedding tears? This day will never come
again and the heron will soon fly. Already,

the light is fading, taking with it all the time
that has ever passed. Let this peace soak

into our skin like medicine, remain with us
long after the heron is gone.

Kingston Mines

Chicago, 2003

He was so feeble they helped
Him to the stage, skin ashy and tough
As elephant hide, a tan suit
And wide-brimmed hat set at a jaunty
Angle. Somebody handed him
A guitar and he held it like a woman

On his lap, tender and reverent
With an edge of possession. You could
See what he used to be, beneath
The scrim of old age, as soon as he started
To play. His fingers found their way
Around that fret like a man revisiting
The street where he grew up—gathering
Speed as he went along. Closing

Our eyes, we could picture ourselves
In summertime, Mississippi—
The sun like a hammer cracking
The ground and heating up young men's
Blood until it ran like lava in their veins,
Pulling them out of their houses
And cars into every kind of trouble.

You knew he was in the thick of it,
Sweat running down his face, his body
Strong and hard as cherry wood. And the hurt
Of losing it all was there in every note,
Like something moaning in the underbrush.
But joy was there, too, as music

Rose from his hands and filled the room
Until anybody who wasn't moving
Had to be dead. And when it was over,
The silence was so profound, it could have
Been the aftermath of a holy man's eulogy—
And you never know, maybe it was.

Geese

Canada geese, after leaving Mallard Lake,
are walking uphill, their webbed feet
like flippers flapping beneath the wetsuit
of their bodies. They move like heavyset
ladies who have lifted their curvaceous
selves from a swimming pool, fulsome
and luscious in their beauty. They walk
in single file as if queuing up for some-
thing so wonderful, it is worth the wait.
But it's the same old grass, the same old
hill, though leaning over it are trees and
from the trees fall leaves through which
the sun shines, turning every leaf to gold.
And the lake they left behind continues
to beckon, so many will soon turn back
to it—its mirrored surface reflecting the
scudding clouds and limbs not yet barren
of their once-bountiful foliage. And all
the while, the geese honk as if they are
irritable drivers stuck in traffic, yet they
can take flight any time, and some do—
leaving behind the hill, the trees, the lake,
their fellow travelers—everything that
holds them to the ground. Because even
when geese fly in formation, each goose
takes off alone, flapping its own wings,
finding its place in a vast expanse of sky
where even a solitary bird separates the
waters above the earth from the waters
below, as necessary and important to this
world as anything God has ever made.

PROCYON

Suppertime

In the narrow galley of her kitchen, my mother
stoops and lifts a wooden cutting board
from the cabinet that won't stay shut,
no matter how hard you close it. Somewhere
in the attic a lazy ghost grins, turns over
in his ghostly bed. So little work to do in an old
house, he thinks. It haunts itself.

She peels an onion, its glistening layers whiter
than the chipped sink they're landing in. A curl
escapes the thick coil of hair pinned
to the top of her head, so she pushes it back
with her wrist. She always was a beauty. Still
is, even in the harsh light that fans across
the cracked ceiling

and pools onto the tiled floor, the last project
my father tackled before life tackled him. He sits
in front of the TV, his chair pulled close
to the screen so he can see it. But the sound
of my mother moving between the stove
and countertop, the clatter of pots and pans,
a paring knife knocking against

the cutting board is, for him, the sweetest music—
better than golf games or touchdowns. Soon,
she'll ask him to set up the folding trays
and he will do it. And as the sun climbs down
from its high horse and the moon readies
itself to hop on—they eat their supper,
the front door left wide open, lamps burning—

a sight so serene, if you happened to pass by
their house, you'd want to come in. So you watch
for a second or two, leash in hand, your dog
whining to move along—remembering a similar
scene from a movie someone you love
once starred in—maybe your own parents,
and some day, if you're lucky, you.

Winter Morning

Beyond the snow-laden hill and ice-covered field, ancient oaks are raising their bare limbs toward a sky marbled with clouds. Gilded by a sun we cannot yet see, they look fixed to the firmament, their shifting so subtle it seems as if these clouds might never move again, as if time itself has stopped and winter has come to stay. I would not mind it. It is cozy here by the fire, watching the day begin through panes of glass, my hair busily turning white, my body grateful for its rest. I never thought of growing older, imagined I would look and feel the same forever. But the decades fly by, and now winter seems to suit me best. There is nothing I need to do and no place to be. A good book is open on my lap, and my husband of thirty years is just up the stairs. I can see the little boy next door already sledding with his mother. He will remember always how it felt to zoom down the steep bank with the person he loves best in all the world—both laughing, faces red from the cold. Meanwhile, oaks that will never again be saplings, hold within themselves the memory of spring. And the winter sky that was, only moments ago, filled with gilded clouds, has at last allowed them to drift ever so slowly away.

Bear Watching in Katmai National Park

Always, there is the cry of gulls, the whistling
of eagles, and the sound of river water

rushing over rocks in the places where sockeye
salmon swim upstream. They jump high

into the air like corn popping in a hot pan,
their silvery bodies glinting like mirrors. No

wonder hungry brown bears heave their furry
haunches out of the long grass, mumbling

and huffing as they make their way to the rapids—
all vying for the best spots. Once there,

they lower their massive heads and wait for fish
to swim by—their hook-shaped claws

designed to pierce a salmon's tasty, neon-pink
flesh. Again and again, the bears pounce

and puncture their prey, tearing strips of meat
from the fish's bones, swallowing the skin.

Then, snout and belly dripping, stomachs full,
they climb the steep riverbank and find

a shady place to dream of fish and more fish—
their silver scales flashing in the sun.

Stairway to Heaven

for my brother

The middle sofa
cushion worked
best, with its two
stiff wedges
of stuffed fabric.
You could brace
both your feet
instead of one,
which skewed
the trajectory
down the long
flight of stairs.
Then you went
sort of sideways
and sometimes
fell off, prematurely.
So, we took turns
with the good
cushion, although
occasionally risked
a single-stirrup ride.
We might have
broken our necks,
of course, but never
did. You waited
a few years to die,
not many—while
I live on and on,
breaking in ways
we never imagined.

The Village Soda Shop

At the Village Soda Shop, the menu was on the wall, and our lunch was served in a paper-lined, plastic basket. Chicken salad was their specialty, and the orangeade, stirred with an extra-long-handled spoon by whoever took your order, was made with crushed ice and real oranges, with enough sugar to keep kids going all day. Among the Soda Shop's loyal customers were the students and professors from a nearby college, men and women on their lunch hours, mothers and grandmothers with children of all ages—so many people, the place was barely big enough, come noon, for everyone who wanted to eat there. We stood in lines that stretched outside a door that looked, when open, like a portal to all the light in the world. It painted the well-trodden floor a pale shade of yellow, shone on the faces of people sitting around the basket-strewn tables—the college students, the parents tenderly wiping their babies' hands and faces—and the rest of us, as lucky as those rays of golden light, just to get in.

Photograph of a Friend

for Malaika

On a gray, cloud-covered morning, a woman
wearing heavy boots, pulls a cart packed with

hay. Her path is strewn with twigs and scuffed
by the heels and wheels of many such journeys

from barn to field. Her copper hair is as vivid
as molten lava against a backdrop of fine mist

rising from a fenced-in pasture. There, a horse
half-hidden by the trunk of a bare-limbed tree,

is nuzzling the damp ground. Its glossy coat is
the color of bark, and its russet tail is whipping

the grass beneath its feet. It won't be long now
before she is close enough to greet this horse

and all the other horses hidden from our view,
her soft voice as familiar to them as a whinny

or whicker. And her hair, bright as a lantern in
this fog-filled photograph, resembles a warm,

steadily approaching light—as if *home* is not
a place, but a person—and soon she will arrive.

Fund Drive

She could be a Norman Rockwell painting,
the small girl on my front porch with her eager
face, her wind-burned cheeks red as cherries.
Her father waits by the curb, ready to rescue
his child should danger threaten, his shadow
reaching halfway across the yard. I take the
booklet from the girl's outstretched hand,
peruse the color photos of candy bars and
caramel-coated popcorn, pretend to read it.
I have no use for what she's selling, but I
can count the freckles on her nose, the scars
like fat worms on knobby knees that ought
to be covered on a cold day like this, when
the wind is blowing and the trees are losing
their grip on the last of their leaves. *I'll take
two of these and one of those*, I say, pointing,
thinking I won't eat them, but I probably will.
It's worth the coming calories to see her joy,
how hard she works to spell my name right,
taking down my *information.* Then she turns
and gives a thumbs-up sign to her father, who
grins like an outfielder to whom the ball has
finally come—his heart like a glove, opening.

My Mother's Cookie Cutters

I found my mother's red plastic
cookie cutters and put

them in a clear glass jar.
They sit on my kitchen counter,

talking amongst themselves,
mostly about the taste

of sugar, the feel of warm
dough, my mother's soft hands.

Merry-Go-Round

Oh, the thrill of it, to clasp those wooden
withers with your scrawny
legs, to put your feet in the stirrups while
the carousel slowly turns and children
climb on, clamoring for the best ponies.
There is barely time to notice the fancy

scroll-work on the saddle
and the swirl of painted mane before you're

moving faster and faster, clutching
the shiny silver pole as your horse
goes up and down and the carousel circles
round and round. The air

rushes by, pungent with popcorn
and caramel apples,
elephant ears and cotton candy,
as faces in the crowd
blur and blend. On and on,
your steed surges forward, prancing

to the beat of the band organ, *oom pa-pa*,
oom pa-pa, until the squeaky sound

of ancient gears grinding to a halt signals
the final turn and strong arms lift
you from your seat as if you're not a cowgirl
riding the range nor an Arabian knight,
but a child who wants to go-round again.

Massage Therapy

Hour after hour, my daughter labors
in low-lit rooms to calming sounds
of falling rain, flute music, or ocean
waves, kneading the flesh of strangers.
Her hands, coated with fragrant oils,
glide over aching muscles, her dark
hair framing her face like the folded
wings of a black swan, her attention
laser-focused on a client's latissimus
dorsi, trapezius, and rhomboids, labels
new to most. But we all know where
it hurts, how unkind words, jobs that
went to someone else, the loves we
have lost—lodge in our lower backs
and shoulder blades, our sore necks
and tight tendons. And we know how
good it feels when tension melts away,
the pulse of our pain slowed by some-
one who moves through this world like
a sun, sharing her warmth and her light.

Luncheon in Paris

It looked like a celebration, but perhaps they celebrated
every day,
she in her red beret, he in his black cap.
They had a feast of soufflés
from entrée to dessert,
as if they would rather dine on air,

but chose a clever substitute. Every so often he stroked
her cheek or took her hand.
She laughed with her head thrown
back and throat exposed, akin to a young girl,
flirting. They spoke like conspirators

with no desire to spoil the surprise for anyone else.
And after they paid the check, he reached
for his cane, she took his arm,
and they strolled down the sidewalk of the
Rue de Castiglione like gracious owners of the property.

Ironing Clothes Three Months After My Father's Death

A friend says *no one irons, anymore*,
but I love the glide of metal over fabric,
how every wrinkle disappears beneath
my hand, like magic. I remember that
dark, wood-paneled room where I ironed
my father's dress shirts, with *American
Bandstand* blaring from the TV—how
the dancers seemed *hipper* than I would
ever be in their platform shoes and mini-
skirts, the boys flailing their arms every
which way, miraculously missing their
partners' faces. I didn't know anything—
how to dance, how to kiss or be kissed,
or what it cost my father to work all day
wearing those stiff, hard-collared shirts
so tough to iron, it took me several songs
to get the creases out. I resented wasting
my Saturdays on such a boring task. I
wanted to go where those couples on TV
were dancing—or anyplace, as long as
it wasn't home. Yet, decades later, the
iron sliding across my linen pants with
puffs of hot steam rising from its water-
laden belly, what I want, if only for an
hour, is to smooth the wrinkles from my
father's shirts, and for him to wear them.

Oak Tree

Leaning over a farmhouse where the same
family has lived for generations,
stands an old oak tree: leaves flapping

harder than wind-blown housecoats hung
on a clothesline—roots rummaging
under the porch for a comfortable pair

of shoes. It spends the days basking
in sunlight, or catching raindrops in each
green palm. In winter, its bare limbs tap, tap

against the darkening sky as it waits
impatiently for snow—its boughs like empty
cradles, rocking. It beckons men

and women from the fields in the evenings,
with branches waving like their mothers used
to do when it was time for supper. And

it comforts them to know that year after year,
this ancient oak keeps watch outside their
little farmhouse, its arms spread wide

over their comings and goings, their weddings
and funerals, births and baptisms, firmly
anchored in the hallowed ground of home.

Bald Eagle

A bald eagle sits on the topmost branch of a white oak tree, wings outstretched, her pale head coppered by the morning sun. Her fledglings are sleeping once again, in the nest. A day and a night in the wild have shown the eaglets how it feels to part from everything they have known, and they are tired. Sounds that were muffled by the cries of siblings and their own high-pitched whistling, were magnified when facing the hours alone—the chatter of smaller birds, the laughter of people on the winding trail below, cars speeding down the distant highway—so much of the world yet to be discovered. But this morning, these three eaglets, so recently fledged, have returned to the bower where they were born, each with a piece of the wide blue sky tucked beneath their wings. And the mother, like mothers everywhere whose children are safe in their beds, can rest.

Yellow Table

Around our chrome and Formica table, in our tiny
two-bedroom, one-bath house on Druid Hills Drive,
our family sat—mother, father, sister, brother—

as history swirled around us like multiple tornadoes
that never touched my brother and me. We passed

the mashed potatoes, chattered about what we had
done all day, lifted our forks from that rectangular

yellow surface with its shiny top and round edges,
and ate what our mother offered. After supper, my

brother and I would leap from our chairs and rush
outside again, in spring, summer, or fall, to lap the

last drops of cream from the bowl of daylight. And
holidays brought cousins and grandparents, turkey,

and pumpkin pie—adding, never subtracting, from
our joy. Nothing terrible happened to us or would

ever happen, as far as we could tell. Yet, I am the
last to remember the bright yellow table, how it lit
our family's faces like comets that circled the sun.

New Day

Though flecks of ice are tap-tapping
at the windows and the ground is frozen over
like a lake in some Northern place
where such things are common, I am lying
in our bed beneath layers of blankets,
my head sinking into a warm pillow. You
have just left the room, closing the door gently
on your way out, thinking I am asleep.
And though there is within me, a deep river
of sadness since my mother's sudden death,
my father's long and painful good-bye,
there is a kind of happiness in the present
moment that sorrow cannot drown.
While we slept, no harm found its way to us.
The moon and stars kept vigil all through
the night—until, awakened from our dreams—
we begin the new day with nothing yet
to show for it save the scent of fresh coffee,
flowing like time into a clean cup.

POLLUX

Cana

Driving to Cana, my mother gripped the steering wheel of her black SUV, the wedding ring she wore for sixty-four years shining in the sun. My father sat beside her, his gaze resting on nothing he could see clearly anymore, but on what he remembered: scudding clouds, the long stretch of highway, cars carrying people he had never met. We engaged in idle talk or traveled in companionable silence—completely at ease in such familiar company. And once we reached the produce store, with its bins and baskets of fresh-picked fruit and vegetables, slippery stacks of vacuum-sealed country ham, jars of hot Chow Chow and clover honey, my mother headed straight for the peaches. Most were at the peak of ripeness and held within their skins the promise of pie. Next, she searched for sweet corn and Better Boys near-to-bursting with flavor. My father, whose sense of taste, unlike his failing eyesight, remained untouched by time, looked forward, already, to supper: thick slabs of sliced tomatoes, crisp cucumbers swimming in apple cider vinegar, corn-on-the-cob glistening with crystals of salt and melted butter—and iced tea with plenty of sugar to wash it all down. I can picture my parents moving from aisle to aisle through that country store—how my mother's face, as she turned to my father, was filled with such light, even a blind man could see it.

Mallard Lake

for Leonard

Here, light falls golden on the wind-rippled water,
and in the water, a branch from a fallen tree—

roots exposed and caked with dirt—has become
a perch for a pair of young cormorants. The backs

of these double-crested birds have been set ablaze
by late afternoon sunshine, their white-feathered

breasts like snow on a north-facing hill. And all
around Mallard Lake, barren limbs from trees still

rooted to the ground, shake from the effort it takes
to bud, and a scudding cloud looks more like a lone

Cheviot sheep searching for its flock. But no people
are in sight, save for the two of us, a long-married

couple marveling at the serenity of such an idyllic
scene. We breathe in the peace of this quiet place—

watch a cormorant open its russet bill and close it
again, as if it, too, is reluctant to make a sound.

IDA

In South Louisiana, every single thing we do is jazz or zydeco.
  –Lauren Daigle

An old woman sits on her front porch in Jefferson Parish, smoking a Kool and watching a copperhead swim past her house. She is wearing her favorite pink housecoat with the torn pocket, and hasn't so much as combed her hair in two days. Three feet above the water line, she is safe from drowning and unwilling to be rescued by a neighbor boy who keeps motoring by in his daddy's fishing boat and won't take *no* for an answer. She was making a roux when the power went out, and left the mess right where it sat since it was clear Ida had no intention of leaving Louisiana without making a big fuss. BeauSoleil was playing Zydeco Gris-Gris on the radio before the room went silent, and that song keeps rattling around her head while a red, high-heeled shoe lodges against a limb rising from the torrent, its branches like the fingers of an arthritic hand. Laughing out loud, she blows a few puffs of smoke into the muggy air, recalling a time when most men would have paid cash to see Rosaline Mayeaux in red stilettos and nothing else. She squints in the bright sunshine as that stubborn boy steers the same old fishing boat up to her porch for what she hopes will be his final run, and hollers like she is deaf, "You about ready to hit the road, Miz Mayeaux?" which says it all when it comes to how much brain power he has going for him, since no roads are visible after Hurricane Ida turned their hometown of Jean Lafitte into a bowl of hot soup.

Poem for My Brother Who Died at Twenty

I picture you sometimes as a man
of sixty instead of the long-haired

boy wearing blue jeans and a plaid
shirt, grease under your fingernails

from fixing a friend's car. I imagine
you fixing me, too, just by sitting

in my sunroom on a warm summer
day—your hair streaked with gray,

laugh lines as thin as threads around
your eyes grown more wise and even

kinder with age. And you are still so
gentle, I can tell, with broken things.

The Neighbors' Barn

It's as if the nice couple down the road
has captured the dark and is keeping it
in their barn. Any moment it could bolt
through the loft's window-like opening
where it can observe, hour after hour, the
light of day. Yet it remains, in as black-
a-breach as there ever was, undaunting
to owls and swallows that swoop in and
out of what seems like a gaping wound.
It is the utter darkness of sealed caves
and underground burrows, where the
creatures we seldom see spend their day-
time hours. We want to shy away from
its inky, one-eyed stare—so incongruent
with the whitewashed boards and gently
swaying branches of the pine trees that
surround it. But it draws us in like black
holes in space from which nothing, not
even light, can escape. So, we have be-
come accustomed to looking elsewhere—
following the sun's blazing path across
the sky or gazing fondly at the little boys
playing next door, their brightly colored
toys strewn around the yard. And when
the night falls across the neighbors' barn
like the shadow of some great nocturnal
bird, we forget it was ever there at all.

Boogie-Woogie

Nobody taught our father to play,
but he could crank out a boogie-woogie
beat on his sister's piano,

fingers bouncing on the keys like ten
happy children, feet tapping—
smiling

like he never did before he left for work
or came home, tired. He'd curl up
on the couch,

loosen his belt—become so still
in sleep, you'd think
he wasn't breathing. But Dad could fly

across a keyboard—his body so light,
we put our hands on his shoulders
to keep him on the ground.

The Sam White Special

My great-grandfather, as a young married man, was already an Elder in the church, toiling weekdays at the sawmill. Come evening, he was bone tired and covered in the dust of dangerous labor, but his work was far from done. By the light of an oil lamp, Papa set up shop in a back room of his house, where men would sit in one of Granny's good ladderback chairs and get their hair cut. It never mattered to Papa's customers that his mirror was cracked in two, and reflected a distorted image. They got what they came for—a decent haircut from a fellow with no barber training and sawdust on his shoes. With a steady hand and a fair price or barter, my great-grandfather was even busier than he wanted to be. Many hardworking sawmillers sported the Sam White Special, which was better than uneven hunks of hair that could swing into a man's eyes when he was inches from a sharp blade. But what kept them coming back was how telling Papa their sins and secrets felt like being baptized in a river—where every dusty soul is washed clean.

Madison's Picture

In Madison's picture, I am smiling.
My hair is long and flying out,

like a dog's ears from the window
of a car, zooming down a highway.

With arms wide open, I have a bright
red apple in one hand and a blue

balloon in the other. There is a yellow
bird with an orange beak perched

on my hip, and I am wearing pink
shoes, my toes pointed, like a ballerina.

Green grass grows beneath me, but my feet
don't touch the ground, as if she drew

me in mid-jump. There is a flower
with ten purple petals, and a round,

yellow sun in the corner of the page,
with a single ray touching my outstretched

hand, (the one holding an apple).
It seems she captured me, with her box

of crayons and earnest concentration,
on the happiest, best day I ever had,

and gave it back to me as a gift—
even better than I remembered.

Fawn

A newborn fawn follows its mother across a steep
hill. The round dots on its reddish-brown body
are as white as cotton, and its pins are as spindly

as the slender-reeded legs on an antique table.
It wobbles as it walks, unaccustomed to moving
itself forward. Even the dull light of dusk must

seem dazzling to eyes that have known only darkness. And how strange the slight breeze must feel,
blowing across its dappled fur. Everything is new—

the trees, the tall grass, the woman standing still
and nearly breathless as the fawn makes its way
to the hilltop, its spots like multiple moons rising.

When I'm with You

It's like I'm eight years old, sitting in the back
of a moving car, my feet hanging out the window

with the hot wind blowing on my toes
and shinnying up my legs and face and tangling
my hair. There's a cooler in the trunk filled

with fried chicken, deviled eggs, and fresh tomato
sandwiches slathered with mayonnaise,
and bottles of Orange Crush hidden under the ice.
We'll stop for lunch halfway to the beach,
too soon to feel the salt
in the air, but close enough to imagine it.

There's a blue bucket with a yellow
shovel that I can't keep from touching

and a shower curtain smell from an inflatable
raft folded in a paper bag on the floorboard.

The people I love most are with me
so the world is as safe as a blanket tucked under
my chin and happiness is something
I expect, like birthday cake.

Road Crew

Beneath a solitary tree, the men and women
on the road crew eat their lunch. They gather
around this cool patch of earth like cowboys
vying for the best spot beside a campfire—
though it's the land outside their shaded circle
that burns. Nearly knee to knee, they chew
without speaking, their angular faces glistening
with sweat, their clothes streaked with dirt.
You wonder if they dream of traffic cones
and angry, honking drivers—feel, even in sleep,
the scalding heat and red dust rising from the road
as cars crawl by them with their air-conditioners
cranked up, windows rolled tight. Come noon,
however, they trade their hard hats for a soft
canopy of leaves, their hard work for a few minutes
of leisure. Like irises soaking up rainwater,
these blue-jean-clad laborers quench their thirst
and feed their hunger, indifferent to the staring
hordes of people passing by. What matters
is the sheltering shade, the bread in their hands,
and a shared sense of common purpose.

For My Daughter, Turning Forty

I can't believe
that you, my little
black-capped
chickadee, my
golden-cheeked
warbler, are
turning forty.
Not too long ago,
you felt so light
in my arms,
I thought you
were hollow-
boned—that you
might fly before
you walked. Now
you're as solid
as a quartz
countertop. And
some days, just
the sound of your
voice carries me.

Pigeons

As the day star rises over a frozen field,
kissing the roofs of houses, the barren

limbs of pin oak trees and the long arm
of the church spire reaching toward the

wintry sky, I can't help but think of the
rock pigeons we saw huddled wing-to-

wing early last evening, on two ropes of
electrical wire. We passed by them so

quickly, I only glimpsed these dozens of
dozing birds, though long enough to note

their cozy coexistence, their companion-
able willingness to keep each other warm.

Heads tucked into their necks, their chests
puffed like rising pastries, most slept but

a few, perhaps keeping watch, remained
vigilant. Like twin strings of black pearls,

they enhanced the beauty of the bright
firmament that would soon fold them into

its purpling light—their little bird hearts
beating as one through the cold, dark night.

Another Memory of My Mother's Kindness

At the end of our street
was a small patch of land
where a neighbor's
grandfather, his body bent
as a boomerang, tilled
the ground and planted seeds.
At harvest time, the sun
beat down hard as rain
and mottled his bare back,
cupped like a hand over rich
swells of dirt and the foliate
flare of ripe cabbages.
Come noon, he'd lean against
a shade tree and drink
the tall glass of lemonade
my mother always brought
him, sowing seeds of her
own while we watched—
and remembered.

Ode to My New Toaster

The same light green as mint chocolate chip ice cream, the new toaster, with its rounded edges and extra-wide slots, sits on the counter alongside a tall vase with painted irises and a container of lemon-scented, liquid soap. You can't help but note its exhilaratingly minty and nearly edible-looking surface, how superior in color and design when compared to the coffee maker, can opener, and the boxy stainless-steel, gunmetal-gray appliances. It is so cool and satiny smooth, I wonder why it doesn't melt in the heat of its own electric energy—so shiny, it almost looks wet. But each piece of my toasted bread, thanks to the instructions with pictures of toast in every shade of brown, (as well as how to achieve it), is as dark as I desire, every single time. And whenever I walk by my new toaster, I appreciate its verdant beauty, its ability to give me what I want the way I want it, and how present it feels when so much has slipped from my hands.

Play Ball

Beneath the artificial lights,
our mothers looked like movie stars
with their red lipstick and shirts that tied

at the waist, waving cigarettes
in the air like conducting batons.
Our fathers broke their concentration
from time to time, smiling at them

like teenage boys spotting their dates
across a high school gym. They would spit
on their hands and wield a bat until

the resounding crack propelled
them to first base, their feet churning red
dust that stained their clothes and rose
in clouds as if they were magicians

in a disappearing act. Our mothers
whistled and cheered no matter what

their husbands did, while we chased
lightning bugs and darted under

the bleachers. As dusk folded into
dark, children gathered in the stands,
leaning against each other like puppies

in a basket until the game ended
and we were packed in the backseats
of assorted family cars. Full of root beer

and hotdogs, sunburned and played out,
we were lulled to sleep by the murmur
of our parents' voices, the night air
rushing over half-rolled windows,

and the spin of our perfect world,
heading towards home plate.

Geminids

for Camille Thomas

We sat outside as the clocks ticked toward midnight
and darkness pressed down upon our grieving world

with soft palms. Which of these stars—I wondered—
are my mother, father, brother, and all the rest who

are gone, never to return. And then, a flock of wild
geese flew above our heads. We heard the beating

of their wings, their persistent honking—yet could
not see their feathered bodies hurtling over roofs

and steeples, the bare branches of a poplar. But we
saw meteors, one after the other, appear and vanish—

witnessed their silent falling. All day long, I listened
to "Dance of the Blessed Spirits" played by a cellist

to empty rooms. I want to hear it play again when
I am dying. May departing souls, traveling through

space like comets, remember how it felt to be alive—
how even birds, flying in the dark, cry out with joy.

Bibliography of New & Selected Poems

New Poems

Night Talks
Night Fishing on Long Beach Pier
The Letter
Goldfinch
Poem by a Woman with Glaucoma
Late Summer Blues
Sorrow Bird
Laundry Day
Girl with a Red Ribbon
The Referee
Stan's Place
A Nimble Deer
The White Bench
Gardening Lesson
Nighthawks
Hate Crime
At the Poultry Show
The Physics of Fishing
The Peony
Breakfast with My Parents
Bare Tree in the Afternoon
The Doctor Who Dies of the Coronavirus After
 the Hospital Runs Out of Gloves
Sunrise Avenue
Estaleen
Sugar
Papa's Chair
Portrait of Elizabeth
At the Cosmetic Counter
Sabine LeBlanc
Sundays
My Father's Cowboy Boots
Alvin and Ila
Egg Salad

In the Midst of Grief, a Heron
Winter Morning
Bear Watching in Katmai National Park
The Village Soda Shop
Photograph of a Friend
My Mother's Cookie Cutters
Ironing Clothes Three Months After My Father's Death
Bald Eagle
Yellow Table
New Day
Cana
Mallard Lake
Ida
Poem for My Brother Who Died at Twenty
The Neighbor's Barn
The Sam White Special
Fawn
For My Daughter, Turning Forty
Pigeons
Ode to My New Toaster
Geminids

Selected Poems

Thread Count (AuthorHouse, 2006)

Autumnal Equinox
Brilliant Delusion
Brown Dress
Kingston Mines
Luncheon in Paris
Play Ball
Rain
Thread Count
When I'm with You
Wisteria

Telling Tales of Dusk (Press 53, 2009), #23 on the Poetry Foundation Contemporary Best Sellers List in 2010

Another Memory of My Mother's Kindness
A Rancher Buries His Wife
Betty's Roadside Diner
County Fair
Madison's Picture
Merry-Go-Round
Oak Tree
Queen Anne's Lace
Stairway to Heaven
Tomato Sandwich

In the Palms of Angels (Press 53, 2011), Winner of a Nautilus Silver Book Award for Poetry, the Gold Medal for Poetry in the 2012 Next Generation Indie Book Awards, and Finalist for the 2013 International Book Award for Poetry

At the Drive-In
Boogie-Woogie
Cling Peaches
Empathy
Heaven
Making the Biscuits
Road Crew
Shrimp Boat Captain
Sponge Bath
To My Brother, Who Died a Virgin

A Lake of Light and Clouds (Press 53, 2014), Finalist for the 2015 USA Best Book Award for Poetry

At the Bowling Alley
Bluebird
Frank and Alice: A Love Story
Hospital Parking Lot
Ice Cream Truck

Kenmore
Loretta Wray
Red Tractor
Slave Cemetery
Stevie Santos

Becoming the Blue Heron (Press 53, 2017), Finalist for the 2018 International Book Award for Poetry

After the Explosion
Angel
Bloom
Fund Drive
Lightning Bugs
Moon Walk
Pixie Cut
Sheller
Suppertime
Washing Dishes

A Sun Inside My Chest (Press 53, 2020), Winner of the 2021 International Book Award for Poetry

Albino Opossum
Fog
Free Breakfast
Geese
Loving You Burns Like Shingles
Massage Therapy
New Bathing Suit
Soleá
The Old Barn
The Ophthalmology Specialists' Secondary Waiting Room

Personal Acknowledgments

Thank you to God for His love and mercy—and for my great-grandparents, grandparents, parents (Tom & Loretta Kirby), brother (Tommy), and other family members and friends who are no longer with us, all of whom I love and miss so much.

I am grateful, also, for the family and friends whose love and support continue to sustain me—especially my husband, Leonard, my daughter, Gia, son-in-law, Brandon, and my uncle, artist Stephen White, whose gorgeous paintings grace the covers of all my books.

Special thanks to beloved friends, Maricam and Johnny Kaleel, whose enthusiasm for life is a daily inspiration, and to the late Frances Y. Dunn, my adored and joy-filled friend, who made the most of every moment of her 103 years on this earth.

I'd also like to acknowledge the Poetry Foundation and my favorite poet, former U.S. Poet Laureate Ted Kooser, who, along with assistant editor Pat Emile, featured poems of mine and so many others in "American Life in Poetry." It was a thrill and an honor every time.

A huge thanks to my publisher Kevin Watson of Press 53, the Press 53 staff, and to Clyde Edgerton, Donna Hilbert, and David Kirby, who took time to write such lovely blurbs for *Night Talks*.

And finally, thank you, dear readers, for reading and supporting my work. It means more to me than I can say.

Terri Kirby Erickson is the author of six previous collections of poetry. Her work has received multiple honors, including the Joy Harjo Poetry Prize, Nautilus Silver Book Award, Atlanta Review International Publication Award, International Book Award for Poetry, Gold Medal in the Next Generation Indie Book Awards, Nazim Hikmet Poetry Award, and many others. Her poems have appeared in "American Life in Poetry," *Annals of Internal Medicine*, *Asheville Poetry Review*, *JAMA*, *Latin American Literary Review*, *NASA News & Notes*, *Poet's Market*, *Sport Literate*, *The Christian Century*, *The SUN*, *The Writer's Almanac*, *Verse Daily*, and numerous other literary journals, anthologies, newspapers, and magazines. She lives with her husband in North Carolina.

Cover artist **Stephen White** specializes in figurative paintings done on wood in gold leaf and transparent oil glazes. His work has been sold worldwide and can be found in many private and public collections, including the Museum of Modern Art in New York City. New work is currently available at City Art Gallery in Greenville, North Carolina.

www.ingramcontent.com/pod-product-compliance
Lightning Source LLC
Chambersburg PA
CBHW030141170426
43199CB00008B/156